CHRISTMAS TREASURES

FRA ANGELICO. *Nativity*. Panel from the Annunziata Silver Chest.
c. 1450. Museo di San Marco, Florence. Photograph: Scala/Art Resource, N.Y.

CHRISTMAS TREASURES

EDITED BY

Deborah Cannarella

BEAUX
ARTS
EDITIONS

CONTENTS

THE STORY OF CHRISTMAS

THE SPIRIT OF CHRISTMAS

SONGS AND CELEBRATIONS

A CHILD'S CHRISTMAS

O TANNENBAUM— HOME FOR THE HOLIDAYS

INTRODUCTION

THE SEASON OF CHRISTMAS is laden with meanings—ancient and modern, sacred and secular—an intermingling of historic facts, religious teachings, folk customs and legends, and the imaginative creations of artists, writers, poets, and musicians.

The essence of Christmas is the birth of Jesus Christ, the founder of Christianity, who according to the New Testament was born in Bethlehem to the carpenter Joseph and Mary, a pious young woman selected by God. What little we know about the event comes from the Gospels of Matthew and Luke. Built on the foundation of these few Biblical passages, the season of Christmas has evolved into the holy and spirited world-wide celebration that we know today. Through the centuries, artists such as Giotto, Brueghel, and Chagall, Bach and Handel, Shakespeare, Milton, and William Carlos Williams have embellished the few facts with imagery and import to convey their own visions of the Nativity. The place in which Jesus was born becomes in paintings a stable, grotto, or temple. The Magi, whose number, names, and origins are unknown, become the three kings Melchior, Gaspar, and Balthazar bearing gold, frankincense, and myrrh. Sheep and oxen, sometimes with the power to speak, encircle the Christ Child in worship, and choirs of angels fill the skies. The pictures we carry of Christmas Day are composites of nearly 2,000 years of artists' imaginings.

Similarly, the Christmas rituals and traditions that we observe reflect beliefs and practices that have evolved over time. The date itself has a long and significant history. The date of Jesus' birth is not recorded in any document. About the year 320, the Church in Rome, attempting to unify the observance of this important event, assigned December 25 as the Feast of the Nativity. As this date closely coincided with the popular pagan Roman celebration of the winter solstice (or Yule), the Church effectively replaced the pagan focal point of worship and festivity with a Christian one. In 529, Emperor Justinian prohibited work and public business on Christmas Day, establishing it as a civic holiday. In 567, the Council of Tours established the practice of fasting through the period of Advent (beginning four Sundays before Christmas) to prepare for the holy day, and proclaimed the twelve days between Christmas and the Feast of the Epiphany (January 6, celebrating the visit of the Magi) as a sacred season.

By 1100, Christmas was an important church feast throughout Europe, but the formal religious observances were abstract and inaccessible to the common people. Francis of Assisi, born in 1182, wanted to remind people of Jesus' humble beginnings and to bring Christmas to the common people. He arranged a reenactment of the night in Bethlehem at his church in Greccio, encouraging worshippers, particularly children, to

gather around the manger and sing to the Child. The tableau, believed to have caused miracles, was repeated every year in Greccio. Other Italian towns soon adopted the custom, which later spread throughout Europe and other parts of the world.

During the twelfth to sixteenth centuries, the people's celebration of Christmas included sacred plays and celebrations performed in churches and homes. Legends, superstitions, and regional customs arose, some of which included a mix of Christian and pagan symbols (recalling the Roman solstice festivals), such as Father Christmas, the Yule log, and mistletoe. The tradition of the Christmas tree is believed to have been inspired by a legend told by the tenth-century geographer Georg Jacob, describing how the night Jesus was born, all the trees in the forest bloomed and bore fruit.

Carols, formerly folk songs associated with dance, also became an important part of the common people's celebration of the season. Among the first composers was Jacopone da Todi (1228–1306) of Italy, who in response to the church's Latin hymns wrote Christmas songs in the common tongue.

During the sixteenth century, the Reformation, a movement that modified doctrines and practices of the Roman Catholic Church and established Protestant churches, spread throughout Western Europe. The celebration of the Mass, holiday processions, and all other forms of Christmas observance were forbidden.

The Puritan sect of England considered Christmas a pagan festival in the guise of a Christian holy day. The rowdy public behavior, excessive eating and drinking, begging, and mockery of authority that characterized the celebrations were deemed to be offenses against God. The singing of carols was particularly offensive.

When the Puritans came to power in England in 1642, their laws prohibited church services and civic festivities on Christmas Day. Businesses stayed open, and people were expected to work. Although town criers reminded citizens, "No Christmas! No Christmas!" the people continued to celebrate, and in 1647, riots broke out in several cities to protest the laws. The restoration of the monarchy in 1660 led to the reversal of the harsh policies against Christmas, although the celebrations then became more revelry than religious observance.

The celebration of Christmas was also illegal in New England during the days of Puritan rule. Between 1659 and 1681, the fine for celebrating Christmas in Massachusetts was five shillings. The day was eliminated from calendars and almanacs, and only those people on the fringes of society—primarily fisherman and mariners—continued to observe the holiday.

In 1681, fearing disapproval from English authorities, Massachusetts revoked its ban on the celebration of Christmas. In the 1750s, the Bay Psalm Book, the hymnal of New England congregations, was revised to include Christmas hymns by the English poets

NICHOLAS POUSSIN. *Adoration of the Shepherds.* The National Gallery, London.
Photograph © The National Gallery, London.

GERARD DAVID. *The Rest on the Flight into Egypt.* c. 1510.
National Gallery of Art, Washington, D.C. Andrew W. Mellon Collection.
Photograph © Board of Trustees, National Gallery of Art, Washington, D.C.

Nahum Tate and Isaac Watts. After 1760, every almanac included mention of Christmas Day. Christmas was again celebrated in the churches, businesses were closed in public observance of the day, and people again filled the streets with revelry and "misrule," but it wasn't until the middle of the nineteenth century that Christmas gained legal recognition as a public holiday in New England.

Nineteenth-century European immigrants brought with them to America their Christmas customs, including gift giving, carols, trees, and crèches—and Saint Nicholas.

Saint Nicholas was a Christian bishop born c. 280 at Patara, in the province of Lycia in Asia Minor. He is the patron saint of seafarers and children, and several legends tell of his miracles. Known for his generosity, Saint Nicholas is said to have dressed in disguise and distributed presents to the poor, especially to children.

When the Dutch settled New Amsterdam (now New York) in 1630, they brought Saint Nicholas (Sinter Klaas) with them. On his feast day, December 6, they carried a statue of the saint in processions down the main streets. By the beginning of the nineteenth century, the St. Nicholas Day celebration had merged with that of Christmas, largely due to the efforts of a group of aristocratic New Yorkers known as the Knickerbockers. Washington Irving's book, *Knickerbocker's History of New York*, published on Saint Nicholas' Day in 1809, mentioned the saint twenty-five times. This New York–born Knickerbocker was the first to make literary mention of Saint Nicholas in this country, which contributed to the popularization of the idea of Santa Claus. Irving's descriptions of quaint celebrations in rural England also helped shape America's notion of "old-fashioned" Christmases.

On December 22, 1822, another New York Knickerbocker, Clement C. Moore, read his children a Christmas poem he had written. "A Visit from St. Nicholas" drew from Irving's tales as well as other sources, including, supposedly, a Dutch friend's memories of stories about the saint. In 1823, the poem was published in the Troy, New York, *Sentinel*. Moore's Saint Nicholas, also referred to as "Santa Claus" and "St. Nick," is a short, round, jolly man with a long white beard. This version of Santa Claus became instantly popular and remains so today.

Thomas Nast, a Bavarian-born American cartoonist, depicted Saint Nicholas many times, integrating his own childhood memories of the saint with Moore's description. As a result of Nast's illustrations, and later Norman Rockwell's, people throughout America conjure up the same character when imagining this benevolent spirit who embodies the message of the first Christmas: peace on earth, goodwill toward men.

In its 2,000 years, Christmas has become a rich mix of sacred and secular celebration. However we observe the day—through singing of carols, family gatherings, or contemplation and prayer—each of us adds to Christmas special meanings of our own.

I

THE STORY OF

CHRISTMAS

The First Christmas

St. Luke 2:1–16

*The story of the birth of Christ was first told
in the New Testament gospels by the evangelists Luke and Matthew
more than two thousand years ago.*

 ND IT CAME TO PASS in those days, that there went out a decree from Caesar Augustus, that all the world should be taxed.

And all went to be taxed, every one into his own city.

And Joseph went up from Galilee, out of the city of Nazareth, into Judea, unto the city of David, which is called Bethlehem (because he was of the house and lineage of David);

To be taxed with Mary his espoused wife, being great with child.

And so it was, that, while they were there, the days were accomplished that she should be delivered.

And she brought forth her firstborn son, and wrapped him in swaddling clothes, and laid him in a manger; because there was no room for them in the inn.

And there were in the same country shepherds abiding in the field, keeping watch over their flock by night.

And, lo, the angel of the Lord came upon them, and the glory of the Lord shone round about them: and they were sore afraid.

And the angel said unto them, Fear not: for, behold, I bring you good tidings of great joy, which shall be to all people.

For unto you is born this day in the city of David a Saviour, which is Christ the Lord.

And this shall be a sign unto you; Ye shall find the babe wrapped in swaddling clothes, lying in a manger.

And suddenly there was with the angel a multitude of the heavenly host praising God, and saying,

Glory to God in the highest, and on earth peace, good will toward men.

And it came to pass, as the angels were gone away from them into heaven, the shepherds said one to another, Let us now go even unto Bethlehem, and see this thing which is come to pass, which the Lord hath made known unto us.

And they came with haste, and found Mary, and Joseph, and the babe lying in a manger.

A Hymn on the Nativity of My Saviour

BEN JONSON

England's first poet laureate Ben Jonson (1572–1637), a contemporary of William Shakespeare, wrote this poem celebrating the birth of Christ. While expressing deep reverence for the fulfillment of the Scriptures, he celebrates the divinity and the humanity of Christ.

 SING THE BIRTH
was born to-night,
The Author both of life and light;
The angels so did sound it.
And like the ravished shepherds said,
Who saw the light, and were afraid,
Yet searched, and true they found it.

The Son of God, th'Eternal King,
That did us all salvation bring,
And freed the soul from danger;
He whom the whole world could not take,
The Word, which heaven and earth did make;
Was now laid in a manger.

The Father's wisdom willed it so,
The Son's obedience knew no No,

Both wills were one in stature;
And as that wisdom had decreed,
The Word was now made flesh indeed,
And took on Him our nature.

What comfort by Him do we win,
Who made Himself the price of sin,
To make us heirs of glory!
To see this Babe, all innocence;
A martyr born in our defence:
Can man forget this story?

Nativity from *Hours of the Duchess of Burgundy*. Ms.76/1362. c. 1450.
Musée Conde, Chantilly, France. Photograph: Giraudon/Art Resource, N.Y.

STEFAN LOCHNER. *Madonna in the Rose Garden.* c. 1450.
Wallraf-Richartz Museum, Cologne. Photograph: Scala/Art Resource, N.Y.

FROM *Even Unto Bethlehem*

HENRY VAN DYKE

Pennsylvanian-born author Henry Jackson van Dyke (1852–1933) was also a Presbyterian minister. This tale, excerpted from "Even Unto Bethlehem," tells the story of Mary's and Joseph's fears and hopes as they decide to travel to the city of David.

F ALL THE HANDICRAFTS in the world there is none cleaner, pleasanter, and more fragrant than that of the carpenter. He works in friendly stuff. If he knows it well enough and can feel its qualities, it yields readily to his working and takes the outward shape of his thought—chair or table or bed, window-frame or shelf or beam.

Well-seasoned lumber he wants, that it may not warp. Knots and cross-grains trouble him, like original sin in man; but he takes note carefully, and avoids or conquers them. He judges his material with his eye before he measures it with square and foot-rule. His mind guides his fingers; his fingers fit his tools; his tools work his will in wood.

What good odors rise around him as he labors! From each tree its own fragrance; the resinous smell of the terebinth and the cypress; the delicate scent of the wild-olive with its smooth, curly texture; the faint, dry sweetness of the orange-yellow acacia with its darker heart; the clean odor of the oak with its hard, solid grain; and on rare days, the aromatic perfume of some precious piece of the cedar of Lebanon, king of trees.

Joseph, the carpenter of Nazareth, was proud of his trade. He loved it. At the beginning of December, on a cloudy morning, he was in his shop making a wedding-chest for the daughter of a rich neighbor. The long box of durable shittim-wood was well smoothed with the plane and firmly mortised with pins of oak; and now on the lid Joseph was working an ornament. With gouge and chisel and file he wrought his design; not of birds or beasts or human figures, for that would have been against the Jewish tradition; but a graceful pattern of a vine with curving branches, broad leaves, and rich clusters of grapes. That was permitted by the law. Was it not even a sacred sign and emblem? Joseph hummed an old song as he carved.

"Blessed is every one that feareth the Lord,
And walketh in his ways.
Thou shalt eat the labor of thy hands;
Happy shalt thou be.
Thy wife shall be as a fruitful vine,
Planted within thy house."

He stood ankle-deep in shavings, absorbed in his task. From the doorway Mary called to him. He looked up.

"Husband, I am going to the village fountain to fill our water-jar. It is empty. There are curious rumors going about among the neighbors. All the other women will be at the fountain. They will tell me the news."

"They surely will," answered the man. "They always know all that is going on, —and sometimes more! But go carefully, beloved. Do not strain to lift the heavy jar."

Gathered around the clear flowing spring, beneath its arch of stone beyond the market-place, Mary found a little crowd of women and girls, filling their jars and pitchers, and talking volubly together. From them she gathered all the gossip. At last came the bit of news, which she had feared.

They looked at her curiously and with those sidelong glances which women always wear when they have been talking about you before you came. But they were kind to her. There was even a shade of pity in their look as they told the news which had a special meaning for her. They helped her to lift her jar of water and balance it on her shoulder. Then she walked home with faltering steps under her burden.

Joseph met her at the door. He took the jar from her shoulder and set it within the house.

"What is it?" he asked. "Why are you so sad?"

"It is bad news, Joseph," she answered, "and it must be true, because it was the wife of the teacher who told me. A decree has gone out from the great heathen man at Rome—the one they call Caesar—that all the world must be enrolled for the payment of a new tax. The governor of Syria has proclaimed it, and that vile king, Herod the Idumean, has ordered it to be done. All the people must be written down in the lists in their own cities, according to Jewish law, by tribes and families. Oh, Joseph, do you see what that means for us? We must go to Bethlehem, the city of the family of David. I am terribly afraid of that long, hard journey now, with my time so near. What if we should run into some danger? What if an accident should befall me? What if I should lose the child I carry, the hope of Israel? I could not bear it. Ah, woe is me! Woe is me!"

She was shaken with grief as she sank upon the bench. The tears rolled down her cheeks, splashing on her dark-red bodice and long blue cloak. The white veil which covered her hair was thrown back in disorder. She was the picture of dismay and sorrow.

Joseph kneeled beside her, distressed and bewildered so that he could hardly speak.

"Listen, dear heart," he stammered, "it may not be so bad. You speak of Jewish law—but this decree is Roman law. Perhaps there is a way out! Our names might be enrolled here in Nazareth—I was born in Galilee—then we could send them to Bethlehem to be registered. What do you think? My friend Matthew in Capernaum is an officer for the Romans—a tax-gatherer—I will go and ask him about it. It is not far to Capernaum! I shall be back soon. Don't be afraid, my wife."

So Mary was a little comforted, and dried her tears. Joseph took his staff and a loaf of bread, and set out for the Lake-that-is-shaped-like-a-Harp.

In his absence Mary was at first very restless and anxious about the result of his journey. On the second day she went into the synagogue and took her place with the women behind the lattice, in the enclosure assigned to them. The speaker for that day was a stranger, a rabbi from Jerusalem. Standing, according to the custom, he read from the book of Prophet Micah.

"But thou, Bethlehem Ephrathah, which art little among the thousands of Judah, out of thee shall One come forth that is to be Ruler in Israel; who goings forth are from of old, from eternity. Therefore will he give them up until the time that she who travaileth hath brought forth; ten the residue of his brethren shall return unto the children of Israel."

JEAN BOURDICHON. *Nativity* from a Book of Hours, Tours, France. M.732, f.31v. c. 1510.
The Pierpont Morgan Library, New York.
Photograph: The Pierpont Morgan Library/Art Resource, N.Y.

Strange words, thought Mary; could they have any special meaning for her? "Bethlehem"? "She who travaileth"? The "Ruler in Israel"? Here was matter that touched her closely.

She listened intently while the preacher, taking his seat now on the bema as was the custom, began to explain the scripture that he had read.

"Bethlehem was David's city. Nowhere else than in this little town can the Messiah, who is to be the son of David, come into the world. 'She who travaileth' is not named. But even now some unknown daughter of Israel may be carrying the Redeemer of God's people hidden under her breast. Wait then, ye faithful, wait patiently, and look with hope to Bethlehem. To Bethlehem first, to Bethlehem only!"

Mary, standing quietly among the women, with her veil drawn down to hide her face, was thrilled to the heart, uplifted, transfigured with a strong joy. Her prayer in time of trouble had been heard. A word direct from heaven had come to her. She herself was the "unknown daughter of Israel."

Her fear vanished. Her path shone clear before her. She lifted her veil from her face, and walked home full of courage and vigor, determined in her duty.

Late that evening Joseph returned from Capernaum, dusty and weary.

"Good news," he cried, "Matthew can arrange it. You can be enrolled here. I may have to go to Bethlehem, but you will stay here, dearest!"

"No, my husband," she answered quietly. "My mind has been changed. A message has come to me straight from heaven. All my fears are gone. My son shall be born in the place where the prophet has foretold his coming. For me, even more than for you, this journey is necessary. You shall never leave me nor forsake me. No harm will come to me. The power of the Most

High has overshadowed me. Let us go even unto Bethlehem. To-morrow I will send a letter to my cousin Elizabeth to meet us there. In Bethlehem it must be."

FROM *The Messiah*

George Frederick Handel's oratorio of arias, recitatives, and choruses was first performed in Dublin, Ireland, on April 13, 1742, to raise money for charity. The libretto is based on the New Testament texts describing the birth, life, and resurrection of Jesus.

EHOLD, a virgin shall conceive,

and bear a son,

and shall call his name Emmanuel,

"God with us."

O thou that tellest good tidings to Zion,

get thee up into the high mountain,

O thou that tellest good tidings to Jerusalem,

lift up thy voice with strength,

lift it up, be not afraid,

say unto the cities of Judah:

Behold your God!

O thou that tellest good tidings to Zion,

arise, shine, for thy light is come,

and the glory of the Lord is risen upon thee.

O thou that tellest good tidings to Zion,

good tidings to Jerusalem,

arise, say unto the cities of Judah:

Behold your God! Behold,

the glory of the Lord is risen upon thee.

BENVENUTO DI GIOVANNI. *The Adoration of the Magi.* c. 1470.
National Gallery of Art, Washington, D.C. Andrew W. Mellon Collection. Photograph © Board of Trustees,
National Gallery of Art, Washington, D.C.

Adoration of the Magi. Stained glass window. Late 15th c. Cathedral, Bourges, France.
Photograph: Giraudon/Art Resource, N.Y.

For behold, darkness shall cover the earth,

and gross darkness the people:

but the Lord shall arise upon thee,

and His glory shall be seen upon thee,

And the Gentiles shall come to thy light,

and kings to the brightness of thy rising.

The people that walked in darkness

have seen a great light.

And they that dwell in the land

of the shadow of death,

upon them hath the light shined.

For unto us a child is born,

unto us a son is given,

and the government shall be

upon His shoulder,

and His name shall be called:

Wonderful, Counsellor, the mighty God,

the everlasting Father, the Prince of Peace.

There were shepherds abiding in the field,

keeping watch over their flock by night.

And lo, the angel of the Lord came upon

them, and the glory of the Lord shone round

about them: and they were sore afraid.

And the angel said unto them:

Fear not, for behold,

I bring you good tidings of great joy,

which shall be to all people.

For unto you is born this day,

in the city of David,

a Saviour, which is Christ the Lord.

And suddenly there was with the angel

a multitude of the heav'nly host,

praising God, and saying:

Glory be to God in the highest,

and peace on earth,

goodwill towards men.

Rejoice greatly, O daughter of Zion!

Shout, O daughter of Jerusalem,

behold, thy King cometh unto thee.

He is the righteous Saviour,

and He shall speak peace unto the heathen.

Then shall the eyes of the blind be open'd,

and the ears of the deaf unstopped;

then shall the lame man leap as an hart,

and the tongue of the dumb shall sing.

He shall feed His flock like a shepherd,

and He shall gather the lambs with His arm;

and carry them in His bosom,

and gently lead those that are with young.

Come unto Him all ye that labour;

come unto Him all ye that are heavy laden,

and He will give you rest.

Take His yoke upon you, and learn of Him,

for He is meek and lowly of heart,

and ye shall find rest unto your souls.

His yoke is easy, His burden is light.

Marc Chagall. *Madonna of the Village*. 1938–42.
Fundacion Coleccion Thyssen-Bornemisza Museum, Madrid.
Photograph: Scala/Art Resource, N.Y.

FROM *On the Morning of Christ's Nativity*

JOHN MILTON

*John Milton, author of the epic "Paradise Lost," wrote this poem in 1629, at
the age of twenty-one, while still a student in Cambridge, England. In this early poem,
Milton celebrates the spiritual essence of the Christian holy day.*

I

THIS IS THE MONTH, and
    this the happy morn,
Wherein the Son of Heaven's eternal King,
Of wedded maid and Virgin Mother born,
Our great redemption from above did bring;
For so the holy sages once did sing,
    That he our deadly forfeit should release
And with his Father work us a perpetual peace.

II

That glorious form, that light unsufferable,
And that far-beaming blaze of majesty,
Wherewith he wont at Heaven's high council-table
To sit the midst of Trinal Unity,
He laid aside; and here with us to be,
    Forsook the courts of everlasting day,
And chose with us a darksome house of mortal clay.

III

Say, Heavenly Muse, shall not thy sacred vein

Afford a present to the infant God?

Hast thou no verse, no hymn, or solemn strain,

To welcome him to this his new abode,

Now while the Heaven, by the sun's team untrod,

  Hath took no print of the approaching light,

And all the spangled host keep watch in squadrons bright?

IV

See how from far upon the eastern road

The star-led wizards haste with odors sweet!

O run, prevent them with thy humble ode,

And lay it lowly at his blessed feet;

Have thou the honor first thy Lord to greet,

  And join thy voice unto the angel choir,

From out his secret altar touched with hallowed fire.

While Shepherds Watched Their Flocks

NAHUM TATE

A new version of the Bay Psalm Book, printed in Boston in 1713, included, for the first time, hymns that told the Christmas story. The original text for this well-known carol was attributed to one of the book's authors, poet and hymnist Nahum Tate (1652–1715).

 HILE SHEPHERDS watched
　　their flocks by night,
All seated on the ground,
The angel of the Lord came down,
And glory shone around.

"Fear not," said he for mighty dread
Had seized their troubled minds
"Glad tidings of great joy I bring,
To you and all mankind.

"To you in David's town this day,
Is born of David's line
The Savior, who is Christ the Lord,
And this shall be the sign.

"The heav'nly Babe you there shall find,
To human view displayed,

All meanly wrapp'd in swathing bands
And in a manger laid."

Thus spake the seraph and forthwith
Appear'd a shining throng
Of angels, praising God, who thus
Address'd their joyful song:

"All glory be to God on high,
And to the earth be peace;
Good will henceforth from heav'n to men
Begin and never cease."

HUGO VAN DER GOES. *The Adoration of the Shepherds*, central panel from the *Portinari Altarpiece*. 1475–76. Galleria degli Uffizi, Florence. Photograph: Erich Lessing/Art Resource, N.Y.

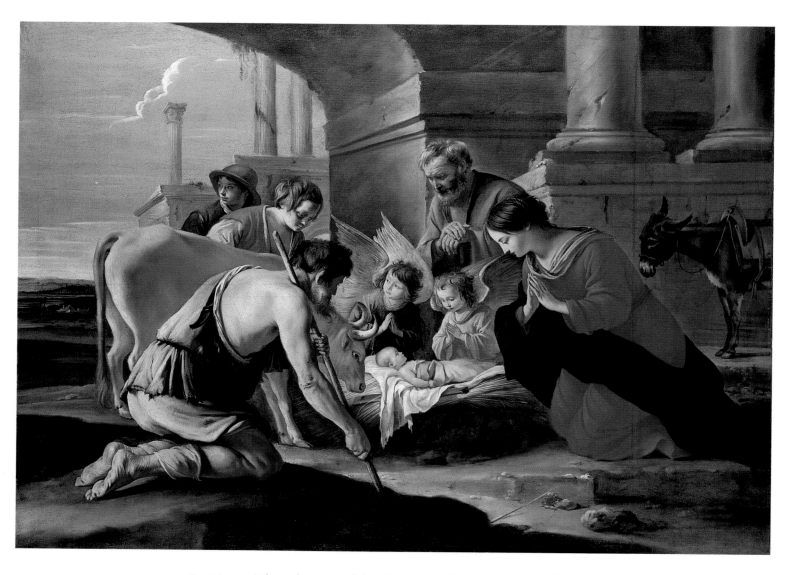

LOUIS LE NAIN. *The Adoration of the Shepherds*. The National Gallery, London.
Photograph © The National Gallery, London.

The Legend of the First Christmas Presents

AXEL HAMBRAEUS

In this tale from Sweden, written in 1950, clergyman and writer Axel Hambraeus
tells the story of three shepherds who, having witnessed the birth of the Christ Child, decide
to return to Bethlehem with gifts for Mary, Joseph, and the baby Jesus.

T WAS THAT NIGHT outside Bethlehem, when the angels had sung about Jesus being born. The three shepherds had returned to their flock. They had a little sheep dog called Tip. He guarded the sheep for them while they took a nap. And it was now the time when they usually slept a while before the sun rose.

But they couldn't sleep at all. They sat talking with one another about the marvelous things that had happened and how they had seen the baby Jesus.

Then one of them said, "Such a poor child he was! And how poor his parents were! I can't forget Joseph. He had such awful shoes. I don't think I've ever seen such shabby shoes. Surely he's walked a long way with them. I seem to recall that I've got a pair of shoes at home; he's welcome to have them."

But the second one said, "I can't forget Mary. Did you see how her cloak was tattered? I saw how she sat freezing in that drafty place, trying to get the cloak around her shoulders, but it was too small, and it was obvious that she was shy about it being tattered whenever visitors came. I think that my wife has a cloak at home that she could have."

"Tattered?" said the third shepherd. "It wasn't tattered at all, it was actually a real fine cloak. But didn't you see that she had had to rip half the cloak to shreds in order to get swaddling clothes for the little baby? I stood all the time looking at the baby Jesus. He had no real swaddling clothes, like those a baby ought to have, beautifully stitched and with red edging: they were his mother's cloak, which she had ripped apart in long strips and swaddled him with. But I seem to recall that at home in the clothes chest we've got swaddling clothes left over since my children were small. I'll give them to the baby Jesus."

And however the three shepherds talked this over, they agreed that they should go home and get the shoes, cloak, and swaddling clothes. And so they patted the sheep dog Tip and told him to guard the sheep carefully while they were gone, and then they were off.

After a while they were back with their things, and then they went in to Bethlehem.

But now there were no angels singing on high, and no light from the heavenly host to lead their way, and they had to walk in the dark, and when they arrived at the town of Bethlehem they were not sure of the way. Previously they had only seen a single road, and it led them straight to the stable, but now there were three roads, and they were all alike.

The first shepherd said, pointing, "I remember quite clearly that it was this way, the one going to the left. I recognize that house over there—we went past it."

"Then you remember wrong," said the second shepherd. "I remember

quite clearly that it's *this* way that goes to the right. I remember a tree standing by the way, and I see it over there."

"No," said the third shepherd, "we should go this way, straight ahead. For there's a well, and we went past that well."

So the shepherds stood there quarreling a long while which way to take, and each of them was sure he was right. And so they decided to go each his own way, and the one who found the baby Jesus should return and tell the others about it.

And so they each went their own way.

The first shepherd went to the left. Past a house and one more and one more, and when he had then gone a piece he caught sight of the stable. He was so sure that he had come the right way that he wanted to run back on the spot and shout for his comrades. But he was a little curious. There was a light shining from the stable window, and he thought, "I can certainly go and look in through the stable window a little bit. I just want to see the baby Jesus, and then I'll run back to my comrades."

But when he looked through the window, there was no baby Jesus. There was an old man sitting on a sheaf of straw, holding a tattered pair of shoes up to the light from the stable lantern. The shoes were so full of holes that the shepherd saw the light straight through them. And he heard the man sighing, "Oh, well, that's the end of these shoes, and I who have such a long way to go."

When the shepherd heard this, he completely forgot that Joseph was to have his shoes. He opened the door and entered the stable.

"I see that you've got such tattered shoes, old man," he said. "I've got a pair of good shoes here; if you want them, then take them."

"Oh, God bless you, my son, God bless you!" said the man, stretching out his hand for the shoes.

At that very instant the shepherd recalled that it was Joseph who should have had the shoes. But he couldn't take his present back now that he saw how happy the old man was with them. He stole out of the stable and went back to the fork in the road.

The second shepherd went to the right. He went past the tree and came to another tree and to still another, and when he had gone a piece he, too, caught sight of a stable. He thought, "I knew very well that I would go the right way. You should always go right; then you can never go wrong."

And he was so sure of himself that he went right into the stable. But then he saw that he had gone wrong.

There was no baby Jesus to be found. But there was a fireplace in one corner of the stable, where an old woman had made a fire from sticks and straw that she had picked up from the stable floor.

"Are you cold, old woman?" said the shepherd. For he was so surprised that he didn't recover in time to say something else.

"Am I cold?" the old woman grumbled. "Shouldn't I be cold in this miserable world, where there's nobody who takes pity on the wretched? Haven't I gone from house to house begging for a cloak to cover myself with, but nobody has given me anything?"

And the shepherd saw that the old woman was trying to cover herself with a cloak so tattered that her bony shoulders and skinny arms were showing right through the holes.

Then the shepherd completely forgot that Jesus' mother Mary should have had the cloak. And he took it and laid it across the old woman's shoul-

HIERONYMUS BOSCH. *Triptych of the Epiphany.* 1510.
Museo del Prado, Madrid. Photograph: Scala/Art Resource, N.Y.

ders. It was a soft and beautiful cloak woven from camel's hair and so warm that the most severe cold couldn't penetrate it.

And the shepherd saw how the old woman's face was transformed when she felt the comfortable warmth across her frozen back. A moment before she had looked really evil and ugly, but now she was almost beautiful, so happy was she.

"Oh," she said. "I had completely lost my faith in God, for I had been asking him so long for help but never got any. But now I know that he lives, since he has sent such a good person to me with this beautiful present." And she clasped her hands, calling out over and over, "Thank you, kind God! Thank you, kind God!"

But then the shepherd all at once recalled that it was Mary who should have had the cloak. What would he get for her now? And while the old woman was sitting at the fireplace thanking God, he stole out of the stable and returned to the fork in the road.

The third shepherd took the way straight ahead. He went past the well. And he went past one more well and one more. "This street could well be called Well Street," joked the shepherd, for he liked a good joke. And he went on a piece, and then he caught sight of a stable.

"To think that I still found the right way!" he said.

There was a light shining through a chink in the door, and the shepherd peeked in through the chink. It gave him quite a start of joy, for inside were indeed the three he was looking for, Mary and Joseph and the child, who was lying in the manger.

But when he entered he saw that he had still gone the wrong way. It was not Joseph and not Mary and not the baby Jesus. They were quite different

people. And it was not even the same stable. He was just about to go away when he saw that the woman was taking her cloak in order to rip it apart for swaddling clothes for the baby lying in the straw, trembling with cold and without anything on its tender little body.

"Stop!" said the shepherd. "Don't rip the cloak apart; I come with swaddling clothes for your little baby."

"Who are you," said the man, "coming to us with such blessed assistance? We didn't expect our baby so soon. We were on the move and found no lodging. And we have no clothes for the baby."

But the shepherd never got to answer his question. He had completely forgotten that it was the baby Jesus who should have had the swaddling clothes. He took them from under his coat, where he had tucked them to keep them warm, and he helped the pale, trembling mother with her white hands to swaddle the little baby in the warm swaddling clothes. The woman wept with joy, kissing her little baby and laying it to her breast in order to give it food. But then the shepherd got shy and went his way.

Slowly he went back to the fork in the road. There stood his comrades waiting for him.

Silent and disappointed, they went back to their flock out in the fields. There the sheep dog Tip came toward them, wagging his tail in friendship. But when he saw they were distressed, he rubbed against them and licked their hands.

And so they put new wood on the fire, wrapping their coats around them and lying down to sleep, after telling Tip to watch closely over the flock.

But when they woke up, they had all three dreamed the same dream.

They had dreamed that Joseph and Mary and the child came to them. Joseph had the new shoes on and Mary the beautiful cloak and the baby Jesus the soft swaddling clothes with the pretty red edging.

When they told this to one another, they sat quietly a long while. Then the first shepherd said, "Maybe, anyway?"

"What, anyway?" said the second.

"Well, maybe we went the right way, anyway."

"Yes, maybe we did," said the third.

FRA ANGELICO. *The Madonna of Humility.* c. 1430/1440. National Gallery of Art,
Washington, D.C. Andrew W. Mellon Collection. Photograph © Board of Trustees,
National Gallery of Art, Washington, D.C.

SASSETTA (STEFANO DI GIOVANNI). *The Journey of the Magi.*
The Metropolitan Museum of Art,
Bequest of Maitland F. Griggs, 1943. Maitland F. Griggs Collection. (43.98.1).
Photograph © 1991 The Metropolitan Museum of Art.

Visit of the Wise Men

St. Matthew 2:1–12

The word "epiphany" means "to manifest." The feast of the Epiphany, January 6, celebrates the visit of the three wise men or kings—Balthazar, Caspar, and Melchior—who brought gifts of frankincense, myhrr, and gold in homage to the Christ Child.

OW WHEN JESUS was born in Bethlehem of Judea in the days of Herod the king, behold, there came wise men from the east to Jerusalem, Saying, Where is he that is born King of the Jews? for we have seen his star in the east, and are come to worship him.

When Herod the king had heard these things, he was troubled, and all Jerusalem with him. And when he had gathered all the chief priests and scribes of the people together, he demanded of them where Christ should be born. And they said unto him, In Bethlehem of Judea: for thus it is written by the prophet, And thou Bethlehem, in the land of Juda, art not the least among the princes of Juda: for out of thee shall come a Governor, that shall rule my people Israel.

Then Herod, when he had privily called the wise men, inquired of them diligently what time the star appeared. And he sent them to Bethlehem, and said, Go and search diligently for the young child; and when ye have found him, bring me word again, that I may come and worship him also.

When they had heard the King, they departed; and, lo, the star, which they saw in the east, went before them, till it came and stood over where the young child was. When they saw the star, they rejoiced with exceeding great joy.

And when they were come into the house, they saw the young child with Mary his mother, and fell down, and worshipped him: and when they had opened their treasures, they presented unto him gifts; gold, and frankincense, and myrrh. And being warned of God in a dream that they should not return to Herod, they departed into their own country another way.

The Adoration of the Kings

WILLIAM CARLOS WILLIAMS

In this poem from Pictures from Brueghel, *inspired by the paintings of sixteenth-century artist Pieter Brueghel, American poet William Carlos Williams describes the painting "The Adoration of the Kings"—and ponders the artist's state of mind as he worked.*

ROM the Nativity

which I have

    already celebrated

the Babe in its Mother's arms

the Wise Men in their stolen

splendor

and Joseph and the soldiery

attendant

with their incredulous faces

make a scene copied we'll say

from the Italian masters

but with a difference

the mastery

of the painting

and the mind the resourceful mind

that governed the whole

the alert mind dissatisfied with

what it is asked to

and cannot do

accepted the story and painted

it in the brilliant

colors of the chronicler

the downcast eyes of the Virgin

as a work of art

for profound worship

JAN BRUEGHEL, THE ELDER. *The Adoration of the Kings.* The National Gallery, London.
Photograph © The National Gallery, London.

In The Bleak Mid-winter

CHRISTINA ROSSETTI

Christina Rossetti (1830–1894) was the sister of pre-Raphaelite poet and painter Dante Gabriel Rossetti and one of the most important women poets in nineteenth-century England. In this Christmas poem, she portrays the event with simple details and human gestures.

N THE BLEAK mid-winter
Frosty wind made moan,
Earth stood hard as iron,
Water like a stone;
Snow had fallen, snow on snow,
Snow on snow,
In the bleak mid-winter,
Long ago.

Our God, heav'n cannot hold him
Nor earth sustain;
Heav'n and earth shall flee away
When he comes to reign:
In the bleak mid-winter
A stable-place sufficed
The Lord God Almighty
Jesus Christ.

Enough for him, whom cherubim
Worship night and day,

A breastful of milk,
And a mangerful of hay;
Enough for him, whom angels
Fall down before,
The ox and ass and camel
Which adore.

Angels and archangels
May have gathered there,
Cherubim and seraphim
Thronged the air:
But only his mother
In her maiden bliss
Worshipped the Belovèd
With a kiss.

What can I give him,
Poor as I am?
If I were a shepherd
I would bring a lamb;
If I were a wise man
I would do my part;
Yet what I can I give him—
Give my heart.

Christmas Carol

KENNETH GRAHAME

*The Scottish essayist and author Kenneth Grahame (1859–1932) was the author of
the beloved fable "The Wind in the Willows." In this simple carol, he sings of winter cold and
the warmth of the Christmas season in the hearts of neighbors and friends.*

VILLAGERS ALL, this frosty tide,
Let your doors swing open wide,
Though wind may follow
    and snow betide
Yet draw us in by your fire to bide:
    Joy shall be yours in the morning.

Here we stand in the cold and the sleet,
Blowing fingers and stamping feet,
Come from far away, you to greet—
You by the fire and we in the street—
    Bidding you joy in the morning.

For ere one half of the night was gone,
Sudden a star has led us on,
Raining bliss and benison—
Bliss tomorrow and more anon,
    Joy for every morning.

EDWARD B. WEBSTER. *The Nativity*. 1956. National Museum of American Art, Washington, D.C.
Photograph: National Museum of American Art, Washington, D.C./Art Resource, N.Y.

FRA ANGELICO and FRA FILIPPO LIPPI. *The Adoration of the Magi*. c. 1445.
National Gallery of Art, Washington, D.C. Samuel H. Kress Collection.
Photograph © Board of Trustees, National Gallery of Art, Washington, D.C.

Good man Joseph toiled through the snow—
Saw the star o'er the stable low;
Mary she might not farther go—
Welcome thatch and litter below!
    Joy was hers in the morning.

And then they heard the angels tell,
"Who were the first to cry noel?
Animals all as it befell,
In the stable where they did dwell!
    Joy shall be theirs in the morning."

II

THE SPIRIT OF
CHRISTMAS

Christmas Bells

HENRY WADSWORTH LONGFELLOW

*American poet Henry Wadsworth Longfellow (1807–1882) wrote this Christmas poem
in 1864, reflecting on the hardships and tragedies of the Civil War. In 1905, the poem was set to
a tune called "Waltham," composed by the English organist John Baptist Calkin.*

 HEARD the bells

    on Christmas Day

    Their old, familiar carols play,

    And wild and sweet

    The words repeat

Of peace on earth, good-will to men!

And thought how, as the day had come,

The belfries of all Christendom

    Had rolled along

    The unbroken song

Of peace on earth, good-will to men!

Till, ringing, singing on its way,

The world revolved from night to day,

    A voice, a chime,

    A chant sublime

Of peace on earth, good-will to men!

Then from each black, accursèd mouth
The cannon thundered in the South,
       And with the sound
       The carols drowned
Of peace on earth, good-will to men!

It was as if an earthquake rent
The hearth stones of a continent,
       And made forlorn
       The households born
Of peace on earth, good-will to men!

And in despair I bowed my head;
"There is no peace on earth," I said;
       "For hate is strong,
       And mocks the song
Of peace on earth, good-will to men!"

Then pealed the bells more loud and deep:
"God is not dead, nor doth He sleep!
       The Wrong shall fail,
       The Right prevail,
With peace on earth, good-will to men!"

Prayer

ROBERT LOUIS STEVENSON

Best known for his adventure tales, such as Kidnapped *and* Treasure Island, *Scottish author Robert Louis Stevenson (1850–1894) here expresses his reverence for the prophesied birth of Jesus and his hopes that its true meaning will inspire our lives.*

OVING FATHER, help us remember the birth of Jesus, that we may share in the song of the angels, the gladness of the shepherds, and the worship of the wise men.

Close the door of hate and open the door of love all over the world.

Let kindness come with every gift and good desires with every greeting.

Deliver us from evil by the blessing which Christ brings, and teach us to be merry with clear hearts.

May the Christmas morning make us happy to be Thy children, and the Christmas evening bring us to our beds with grateful thoughts, forgiving and forgiven, for Jesus' sake. Amen!

FROM *A Christmas Carol*

Charles Dickens

Christmas is a time of family and of feasting. This passage from one of the most loved tales of all time describes how the bounty of Christmas fills the household of Bob Cratchit, his wife, Tiny Tim, and the other children, despite their limited means.

THEN UP ROSE Mrs. Cratchit, Cratchit's wife, dressed out but poorly in a twice-turned gown, but brave in ribbons, which are cheap and make a goodly show for sixpence; and she laid the cloth, assisted by Belinda Cratchit, second of her daughters, also brave in ribbons; while Master Peter Cratchit plunged a fork into the saucepan of potatoes, and getting the corners of his monstrous shirt collar (Bob's private property, conferred upon his son and heir in honor of the day) into his mouth, rejoiced to find himself so gallantly attired, and yearned to show his linen in the fashionable parks. And now two smaller Cratchits, boy and girl, came tearing in, screaming that outside the baker's they had smelled the goose and known it for their own; and basking in luxurious thoughts of sage-and-onion, these young Cratchits danced about the table, and exalted Master Peter Cratchit to the skies, while he (not proud, although his color nearly choked him) blew the fire, until the slow potatoes bubbling up knocked loudly at the saucepan-lid to be let out and peeled.

"What has ever got your precious father then?" said Mrs. Cratchit. "And your brother, Tiny Tim! And Martha warn't as late last Christmas Day by half-an-hour!"

"Here's Martha, mother!" said a girl, appearing as she spoke.

Thomas Falcon Marshall. *Christmas Morning.* Christopher Wood Gallery, London.
Photograph © The Bridgeman Art Library International Ltd., London/New York.

Robert Braithwaite Martineau. *The Christmas Hamper*. Private collection.
Photograph © The Bridgeman Art Library International Ltd., London/New York.

"Here's Martha, mother!" cried the two young Cratchits. "Hurrah! There's *such* a goose, Martha!"

"Why, bless your heart alive, my dear, how late you are!" said Mrs. Cratchit, kissing her a dozen times, and taking off her shawl and bonnet for her with officious zeal.

"We'd a deal of work to finish up last night," replied the girl, "and had to clear away this morning, mother!"

"Well! Never mind so long as you are come," said Mrs. Cratchit. "Sit ye down before the fire, my dear, and have a warm, Lord bless ye!"

"No, no! There's father coming," cried the two young Cratchits, who were everywhere at once. "Hide, Martha, hide!"

So Martha hid herself, and in came little Bob, the father, with at least three feet of comforter exclusive of the fringe, hanging down before him; and his threadbare clothes darned and brushed, to look seasonable; and Tiny Tim upon his shoulder. Alas, for Tiny Tim, he bore a little crutch, and had his limbs supported by an iron frame!

"Why, where's our Martha?" cried Bob Cratchit, looking round.

"Not coming," said Mrs. Cratchit.

"Not coming!" said Bob, with a sudden declension in his high spirits; for he had been Tim's blood horse all the way from church, and had come home rampant. "Not coming upon Christmas Day!"

Martha didn't like to see him disappointed, if it were only in joke; so she came out prematurely from behind the closet door, and ran into his arms, while the two young Cratchits hustled Tiny Tim, and bore him off into the wash-house, that he might hear the pudding singing in the copper.

"And how did little Tim behave?" asked Mrs. Cratchit, when she had ral-

lied Bob on his credulity, and Bob had hugged his daughter to his heart's content.

"As good as gold," said Bob, "and better. Somehow he gets thoughtful, sitting by himself so much, and thinks the strangest things you ever heard. He told me, coming home, that he hoped the people saw him in the church, because he was a cripple, and it might be pleasant to them to remember upon Christmas Day, who made lame beggars walk and blind men see."

Bob's voice was tremulous when he told them this, and trembled more when he said that Tiny Tim was growing strong and hearty.

His active little crutch was heard upon the floor, and back came Tiny Tim before another word was spoken, escorted by his brother and sister to his stool before the fire; and while Bob, turning up his cuffs—as if, poor fellow, they were capable of being made more shabby—compounded some hot mixture in a jug with gin and lemons, and stirred it round and round and put it on the hob to simmer, Master Peter and the two ubiquitous young Cratchits went to fetch the goose, with which they soon returned in high procession.

Such a bustle ensued that you might have thought a goose the rarest of all birds; a feathered phenomenon, to which a black swan was a matter of course—and in truth it was something very like it in that house. Mrs. Cratchit made the gravy (ready beforehand in a little saucepan) hissing hot; Master Peter mashed the potatoes with incredible vigor; Miss Belinda sweetened up the apple sauce; Martha dusted the hot plates; Bob took Tiny Tim beside him in a tiny corner at the table; the two young Cratchits set chairs for everybody, not forgetting themselves, and mounting guard upon their posts, crammed spoons into their mouths, lest they should shriek for goose

before their turn came to be helped. At last the dishes were set on, and grace was said. It was succeeded by a breathless pause, as Mrs. Cratchit, looking slowly all along the carving-knife, prepared to plunge it in the breast; but when she did, and when the long expected gush of stuffing issued forth, one murmur of delight arose all round the board, and even Tiny Tim, excited by the two young Cratchits, beat on the table with the handle of his knife, and feebly cried Hurrah!

There never was such a goose. Bob said he didn't believe there ever was such a goose cooked. Its tenderness and flavor, size and cheapness, were the themes of universal admiration. Eked out by the apple sauce and mashed potatoes, it was a sufficient dinner for the whole family; indeed, as Mrs. Cratchit said with great delight (surveying one small atom of a bone upon the dish) they hadn't ate it all at last! Yet every one had had enough, and the youngest Cratchits, in particular, were steeped in sage and onion to the eyebrows! But now, the plates being changed by Miss Belinda, Mrs. Cratchit left the room alone—too nervous to bear witness—to take the pudding up and bring it in.

Suppose it should not be done enough! Suppose it should break in the turning out! Suppose somebody should have got over the wall of the backyard, and stolen it while they were merry with the goose—a supposition at which the two young Cratchits became livid! All sorts of horrors were supposed.

Hallo! A great deal of steam! The pudding was out of the copper. A smell like a washing-day! That was the cloth. A smell like an eating-house and a pastrycook's next door to each other, with a laundress's next door to that! That was the pudding! In half a minute Mrs. Cratchit entered—flushed, but

smiling proudly—with the pudding like a speckled cannon-ball so hard and firm blazing in half of half-a-quartern of ignited brandy, and bedight with Christmas holly stuck into the top.

Oh, a wonderful pudding! Bob Cratchit said, and calmly too, that he regarded it as the greatest success achieved by Mrs. Cratchit since their marriage. Mrs. Cratchit said that now the weight was off her mind, she would confess she had had her doubts about the quantity of flour. Everybody had something to say about it, but nobody said or thought it was at all a small pudding for a large family. It would have been flat heresy to do so. Any Cratchit would have blushed to hint at such a thing.

At last the dinner was all done, the cloth was cleared, the hearth swept, and the fire made up. The compound in the jug being tasted, and considered perfect, apples and oranges were put upon the table, and a shovelful of chestnuts on the fire. Then all the Cratchit family drew round the hearth, in what Bob Cratchit called a circle, meaning half a one; and at Bob Cratchit's elbow stood the family display of glass. Two tumblers, and a custard-cup without a handle.

These held the hot stuff from the jug, however, as well as golden goblets would have done; and Bob served it out with beaming looks, while the chestnuts on the fire sputtered and cracked noisily. Then Bob proposed:

"A Merry Christmas to us all, my dears. God bless us!"

Which all the family re-echoed.

"God bless us every one!" said Tiny Tim, the last of all.

SOPHIE ANDERSON. *Christmas Turkey*. c. 1877. Private collection.
Photograph © The Bridgeman Art Library International Ltd., London/New York.

FROM *The Adventure of the Blue Carbuncle*

SIR ARTHUR CONAN DOYLE

In this holiday tale, published in 1892 by Sir Arthur Conan Doyle in the British magazine The Strand, *the relentless sleuth Sherlock Holmes is hot on the scent of a Christmas goose with an unusual style of stuffing: the Countess of Morcar's precious blue gem!*

HAD CALLED upon my friend Sherlock Holmes upon the second morning after Christmas, with the intention of wishing him the compliments of the season. He was lounging upon the sofa in a purple dressing-gown, a pipe-rack within his reach upon the right, and a pile of crumpled morning papers, evidently newly studied, near at hand. Beside the couch was a wooden chair, and on the angle of the back hung a very seedy and disreputable hard-felt hat, much the worse for wear, and cracked in several places. A lens and a forceps lying upon the seat of the chair suggested that the hat had been suspended in this manner for the purpose of this examination.

"You are engaged," said I; "perhaps I interrupt you."

"Not at all. I am glad to have a friend with whom I can discuss my results. The matter is a perfectly trivial one"—he jerked his thumb in the direction of the old hat— "but there are points in connection with it which are not entirely devoid of interest and even instruction."

I seated myself in his armchair and warmed my hands before his crackling fire, for a sharp frost had set in, and the windows were thick with the

ice crystals. "I suppose," I remarked, "that, homely as it looks, this thing has some deadly story linked on to it—that it is the clue which will guide you in the solution of some mystery and the punishment of some crime."

"No, no. No crime," said Sherlock Holmes, laughing. "Only one of those whimsical little incidents which will happen when you have four million human beings all jostling each other within the space of a few square miles. Amid the action and reaction of so dense a swarm of humanity, every possible combination of events may be expected to take place, and many a little problem will be presented which may be striking and bizarre without being criminal. We have already had experience of such."

"So much so," I remarked, "that of the last six cases which I have added to my notes, three have been entirely free of any legal crime."

"Precisely. You allude to my attempt to recover the Irene Adler papers, to the singular case of Miss Mary Sutherland, and to the adventure of the man with the twisted lip. Well, I have no doubt that this small matter will fall into the same innocent category. You know Peterson, the commissionaire?"

"Yes."

"It is to him that this trophy belongs."

"It is his hat."

"No, no; he found it. Its owner is unknown. I beg that you will look upon it not as a battered billycock but as an intellectual problem. And, first, as to how it came here. It arrived upon Christmas morning, in company with a good fat goose, which is, I have no doubt, roasting at this moment in front of Peterson's fire. The facts are these: about four o'clock on Christmas morning, Peterson, who, as you know, is a very honest fellow, was returning from some small jollification and was making his way homeward down Tottenham Court

Road. In front of him he saw, in the gaslight, a tallish man, walking with a slight stagger, and carrying a white goose slung over his shoulder. As he reached the corner of Goodge Street, a row broke out between this stranger and a little knot of roughs. One of the latter knocked off the man's hat, on which he raised his stick to defend himself and, swinging it over his head, smashed the shop window behind him. Peterson had rushed forward to protect the stranger from his assailants; but the man, shocked at having broken the window, and seeing an official-looking person in uniform rushing towards him, dropped his goose, took to his heels, and vanished amid the labyrinth of small streets which lie at the back of Tottenham Court Road. The roughs also had fled at the appearance of Peterson, so that he was left in possession of the field of battle, and also of the spoils of victory in the shape of this battered hat and a most unimpeachable Christmas goose."

"Which surely he restored to their owner?"

"My dear fellow, there lies the problem. It is true that 'For Mrs. Henry Baker' was printed upon a small card which was tied to the bird's left leg, and it is also true that the initials 'H.B.' are legible upon the lining of this hat; but as there are some thousands of Bakers, and some hundreds of Henry Bakers in this city of ours, it is not easy to restore lost property to any one of them."

"What, then, did Peterson do?"

"He brought round both hat and goose to me on Christmas morning, knowing that even the smallest problems are of interest to me. The goose we retained until this morning, when there were signs that, in spite of the slight frost, it would be well that it should be eaten without unnecessary delay. Its finder has carried it off, therefore, to fulfill the ultimate destiny of a goose, while I continue to retain the hat of the unknown gentleman who lost his Christmas dinner."

ROMARE BEARDEN. *Adoration of the Wise Men.* 1945. Collection of the Newark Museum.
Gift of Mr. and Mrs. Benjamin E. Tepper, 1946. Inv.46.164.
Photograph: The Newark Museum, Newark, NJ/Art Resource, N.Y.
© Romare Bearden Foundation/licensed by VAGA, New York, N.Y.

The Gift of the Magi

O. Henry

William Sydney Porter (1862–1918) was born in Greensboro, North Carolina, and became a well-known writer of short stories under the pen name O. Henry. Published in 1906, this is the tale of Della and Jim, a young couple whose gifts to each other convey the true spirit of giving.

NE DOLLAR and eighty-seven cents. That was all.

And sixty cents of it was in pennies. Pennies saved one and two at a time by bulldozing the grocer and the vegetable man and the butcher until one's cheeks burned with the silent imputation of parsimony that such close dealing implied. Three times Della counted it. One dollar and eighty-seven cents. And the next day would be Christmas.

There was clearly nothing to do but flop down on the shabby little couch and howl. So Della did it. Which instigates the moral reflection that life is made up of sobs, sniffles, and smiles, with sniffles predominating.

While the mistress of the home is gradually subsiding from the first stage to the second, take a look at the home. A furnished flat at eight dollars per week. It did not exactly beggar description, but it certainly had that word on the lookout for the mendicancy squad.

In the vestibule below was a letter-box into which no letter would go, and an electric button from which no mortal finger could coax a ring. Also appertaining thereunto was a card bearing the name "Mr. James Dillingham Young."

The "Dillingham" had been flung to the breeze during a former period

of prosperity when its possessor was being paid thirty dollars per week. Now, when the income was shrunk to twenty dollars, the letters of "Dillingham" looked blurred, as though they were thinking seriously of contracting to a modest and unassuming D. But whenever Mr. James Dillingham Young came home and reached his flat above he was called "Jim" and greatly hugged by Mrs. James Dillingham Young, already introduced to you as Della. Which is all very good.

Della finished her cry and attended to her cheeks with a powder puff. She stood by the window and looked out dully at a gray cat walking a gray fence in a gray back yard. Tomorrow would be Christmas Day, and she had only $1.87 with which to buy Jim a present. She had been saving every penny she could for months, with this result. Twenty dollars a week doesn't go far. Expenses had been greater than she had calculated. They always are. Only $1.87 to buy a present for Jim. Her Jim. Many a happy hour she had spent planning for something nice for him. Something fine and rare and sterling—something just a little bit near to being worthy of the honor of being owned by Jim.

There was a pier glass between the windows of the room. Perhaps you have seen a pier glass in an eight-dollar flat. A very thin and very agile person may, by observing his reflection in a rapid sequence of longitudinal strips, obtain a fairly accurate conception of his looks. Della, being slender, had mastered the art.

Suddenly she whirled from the window and stood before the glass. Her eyes were shining brilliantly, but her face had lost its color within twenty seconds. Rapidly she pulled down her hair and let it fall to its full length.

Now, there were two possessions of the James Dillingham Youngs in

which they both took a mighty pride. One was Jim's gold watch that had been his father's and his grandfather's. The other was Della's hair. Had the Queen of Sheba lived in the flat across the airshaft, Della would have let her hair hang out the window some day to dry just to depreciate Her Majesty's jewels and gifts. Had King Solomon been the janitor, with all his treasures piled up in the basement, Jim would have pulled out his watch every time he passed, just to see him pluck at his beard from envy.

So now Della's beautiful hair fell about her, rippling and shining like a cascade of brown waters. She did it up again nervously and quickly. Once she faltered for a minute while a tear splashed on the worn red carpet.

On went her old brown jacket; on went her old brown hat. With a whirl of skirts and with the brilliant sparkle still in her eyes, she fluttered out the door and down the stairs to the street.

Where she stopped the sign read: "Mme. Sofronie. Hair Goods of All Kinds." One flight up Della ran, and collected herself, panting. Madame, large, too white, chilly, hardly looked the "Sofronie."

"Will you buy my hair?" asked Della.

"I buy hair," said Madame. "Take yer hat off and let's have a sight at the looks of it."

Down rippled the brown cascade.

"Twenty dollars," said Madame, lifting the mass with a practiced hand.

"Give it to me quick," said Della.

Oh, and the next two hours tripped on rosy wings. Forget the hashed metaphor. She was ransacking the stores for Jim's present.

She found it at last. It surely had been made for Jim and no one else. There was no other like it in any of the stores, and she had turned all of them

Journey of the Magi, Led by the Star; Adoration of the Magi; Return of the Magi.
Page from a Missal, Germany (Abbey of Weingarten). M.710, f.19v. c. 1200–32.
The Pierpont Morgan Library, New York.
Photograph: The Pierpont Morgan Library/Art Resource, N.Y.

inside out. It was a platinum watch-chain, simple and chaste in design, properly proclaiming its value by substance alone and not by meretricious ornamentation—as all good things should do. It was even worthy of The Watch. A soon as she saw it she knew that it must be Jim's. It was like him. Quietness and value—the description applied to both. Twenty-one dollars they took from her for it, and she hurried home with the eighty-seven cents. With that chain on his watch Jim might be properly anxious about the time in any company. Grand as the watch was, he sometimes looked at it on the sly on account of the shabby old leather strap that he used in place of a proper gold chain.

When Della reached home her intoxication gave way a little to prudence and reason. She got out her curling-irons and lighted the gas and went to work repairing the ravages made by generosity added to love. Which is always a tremendous task, dear friends—a mammoth task.

Within forty minutes her head was covered with tiny close-lying curls that made her look wonderfully like a truant schoolboy. She looked at her reflection in the mirror long, carefully, and critically.

"If Jim doesn't kill me," she said to herself, "before he takes a second look at me, he'll say I look like a Coney Island chorus girl. But what could I do—oh! what could I do with a dollar and eighty-seven cents?"

At seven o'clock the coffee was made and the frying pan was on the back stove, hot and ready to cook the chops.

Jim was never late. Della doubled the watch chain in her hand and sat on the corner of the table near the door that he always entered. Then she heard his step on the stair way down on the first flight, and she turned white for just a moment. She had a habit of saying little silent prayers about the

simplest everyday things, and now she whispered: "Please, God, make him think I am still pretty."

The door opened and Jim stepped in and closed it. He looked thin and very serious. Poor fellow, he was only twenty-two—and to be burdened with a family! He needed a new overcoat and he was without gloves.

Jim stepped inside the door, as immovable as a setter at the scent of quail. His eyes were fixed upon Della, and there was an expression in them that she could not read, and it terrified her. It was not anger, nor surprise, nor disapproval, nor horror, nor any of the sentiments that she had been prepared for. He simply stared at her fixedly with that peculiar expression on his face.

Della wriggled off the table and went for him.

"Jim, darling," she cried, "don't look at me that way. I had my hair cut off and sold it because I couldn't have lived through Christmas without giving you a present. It'll grow out again—you won't mind, will you? I just had to do it. My hair grows awfully fast. Say 'Merry Christmas!' Jim, and let's be happy. You don't know what a nice—what a beautiful, nice gift I've got for you."

"You've cut off your hair?" asked Jim, laboriously, as if he had not arrived at that patent fact yet even after the hardest mental labor.

"Cut it off and sold it," said Della. "Don't you like me just as well, anyhow? I'm me without my hair, ain't I?"

Jim looked about the room curiously.

"You say your hair is gone?" he said, with an air almost of idiocy.

"You needn't look for it," said Della. "It's sold, I tell you—sold and gone, too. It's Christmas Eve, boy. Be good to me, for it went for you. Maybe the hairs of my head were numbered," she went on with a sudden serious

sweetness, "but nobody could ever count my love for you. Shall I put the chops on, Jim?"

Out of his trance Jim seemed to quickly wake. He enfolded his Della. For ten seconds let us regard with discreet scrutiny some inconsequential object in the other direction. Eight dollars a week or a million a year—what is the difference? A mathematician or a wit would give you the wrong answer. The Magi brought valuable gifts, but that was not among them. This dark assertion will be illuminated later on.

Jim drew a package from his overcoat pocket and threw it upon the table.

"Don't make any mistake, Dell, " he said, "about me. I don't think there's anything in the way of a haircut or a shave or a shampoo that could make me like my girl any less. But if you'll unwrap that package you may see why you had me going awhile at first."

White fingers and nimble tore at the string and paper. And then an ecstatic scream of joy; and then, alas! a quick feminine change to hysterical tears and wails, necessitating the immediate employment of all the comforting powers of the lord of the flat.

For there lay The Combs—the set of combs that Della had worshiped for long in a Broadway window. Beautiful combs, pure tortoise shell, with jeweled rims—just the shade to wear in the beautiful vanished hair. They were expensive combs, she knew, and her heart had simply craved and yearned over them without the least hope of possession. And now they were hers, but the tresses that should have adorned the coveted adornments were gone.

But she hugged them to her bosom, and at length she was able to look up with dim eyes and a smile and say: "My hair grows so fast, Jim!"

And then Della leaped up like a little singed cat and cried, "Oh, oh!"

Jim had not yet seen his beautiful present. She held it out to him eagerly upon her open palm. The dull precious metal seemed to flash with a reflection of her bright and ardent spirit.

"Isn't it a dandy, Jim? I hunted all over town to find it. You'll have to look at the time a hundred times a day now. Give me your watch. I want to see how it looks on it."

Instead of obeying, Jim tumbled down on the couch and put his hands under the back of his head and smiled.

"Dell," said he, "let's put our Christmas presents away and keep 'em awhile. They're too nice to use just at present. I sold the watch to get the money to buy your combs. And now suppose you put the chops on."

The Magi, as you know, were wise men—wonderfully wise men—who brought gifts to the Babe in the manger. They invented the art of giving Christmas presents. Being wise, their gifts were no doubt wise ones, possibly bearing the privilege of exchange in case of duplication. And here I have lamely related to you the uneventful chronicle of two foolish children in a flat who most unwisely sacrificed for each other the greatest treasures of their house. But in a last word to the wise of these days let it be said that of all who give gifts these two were the wisest. Of all who give and receive gifts, such as they are the wisest. Everywhere they are the wisest. They are the Magi.

CURRIER & IVES. *Central Park, Winter. The Skating Pond.* Undated.
Museum of the City of New York. The Harry T. Peters Collection.

FRANK DADD. *A Merry Christmas*. Illustration from the Pears Christmas Annual, 1907.
A&F Pears Ltd., London. Photograph © The Bridgeman Art Library International Ltd., London/New York.

Christmas Trees: A Christmas Circular Letter

ROBERT FROST

One Christmas, American poet Robert Frost (1874–1963) and his children made a homemade card. Frost wrote out this poem longhand above the children's sketch, telling of a man who, faced with the prospect of selling his fir trees, wishes he could send one to a friend.

THE CITY had withdrawn into itself

And left at last the country to the country;

When between whirls of snow not come to lie

And whirls of foliage not yet laid, there drove

A stranger to our yard, who looked the city

Yet did in country fashion in that there

He sat and waited till he drew us out,

A-buttoning coats, to ask him who he was.

He proved to be the city come again

To look for something it had left behind

And could not do without and keep is Christmas.

He asked if I would sell my Christmas trees;

My woods—the young fir balsams like a place

Where houses all are churches and have spires.

I hadn't thought of them as Christmas trees.

I doubt if I was tempted for a moment

To sell them off their feet to go in cars

And leave the slope behind the house all bare,

Where the sun shines now no warmer than the moon.

I'd hate to have them know it if I was.

Yet more I'd hate to hold my trees, except

As others hold theirs or refuse for them,

Beyond the time of profitable growth—

The trial by market everything must come to.

I dallied so much with the thought of selling.

Then whether from mistaken courtesy

And fear of seeming short of speech, or whether

From hope of hearing good of what was mine.

I said, "There aren't enough to be worthwhile."

"I could soon tell how many they would cut,

You let me look them over."

    "You could look.

But don't expect I'm going to let you have them."

Pasture they spring in, some in clumps too close

That lop each other of boughs, but not a few

Quite solitary and having equal boughs

All round and round. The latter he nodded "Yes" to,

Or paused to say beneath some lovelier one,

With a buyer's moderation, "That would do."

I thought so too, but wasn't there to say so.

We climbed the pasture on the south, crossed over,

And came down on the north.

He said, "A thousand."

"A thousand Christmas trees!—at what apiece?"

He felt some need of softening that to me:

"A thousand trees would come to thirty dollars."

Then I was certain I had never meant

To let him have them. Never show surprise!

But thirty dollars seemed so small beside

The extent of pasture I should strip, three cents

(For that was all they figured out apiece)—

Three cents so small beside the dollar friends

I should be writing to within the hour

Would pay in cities for good trees like those,

Regular vestry-trees whole Sunday Schools

Could hang enough on to pick off enough.

A thousand Christmas trees I didn't know I had!

Worth three cents more to give away than sell

As may be shown by a simple calculation.

Too bad I couldn't lay one in a letter.

I can't help wishing I could send you one,

In wishing you herewith a Merry Christmas.

FROM *The Christmas Box*

Richard Paul Evans's poignant story of a young father
finding the true meaning of Christmas in the eyes of his young daughter
was written for his own three daughters.

SET THE LETTER back in the box and pulled my knees into my chest, burying my head into my thighs. My mind reeled, as if in a dream, where pieces of the day's puzzle are unraveled and rewoven into a new mosaic, defying the improbability of the cut edges fitting. Yet they did fit. The meaning of Mary's question was now clear to me. The first gift of Christmas. The true meaning of Christmas. My body and mind tingled with the revelations of the day. Downstairs I heard the rustling of Keri's return. I walked down and helped her in.

"I came back to get Jenna some dinner," she said, falling into my arms. "I'm so exhausted," she cried. "And so sad."

I held her tightly. "How is she?"

"Not very good."

"Why don't you lie down, I'll put some soup on and get Jenna ready for bed."

Keri stretched out on the sofa while I dressed Jenna, fed her, then carried her downstairs to the den.

It was dark outside and in absence of a fire, the room was bathed by the peaceful illumination of the Christmas tree lights. Strands flashed on and

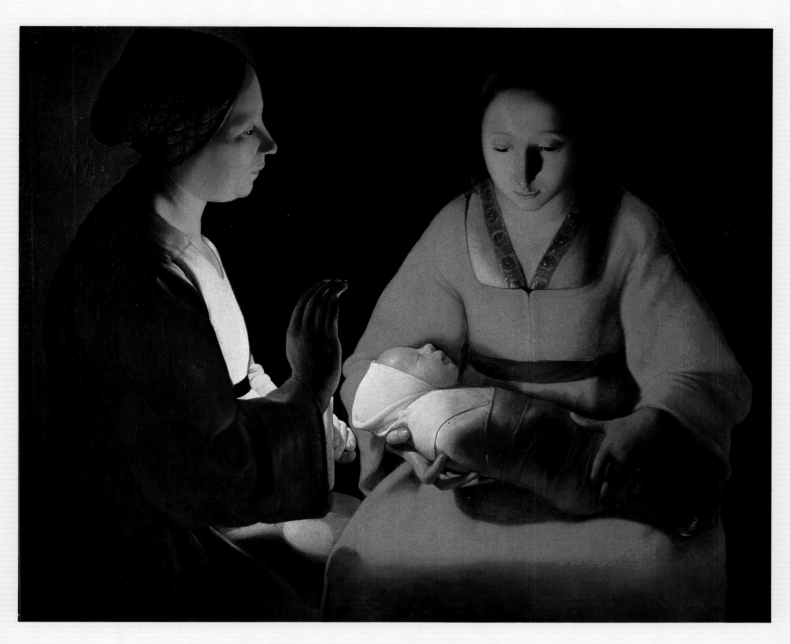

GEORGES DE LA TOUR. *Nativity*. Musée des Beaux-Arts, Rennes, France.
Photograph: Erich Lessing/Art Resource, N.Y.

off in syncopation, casting shadows of different shapes and hues. I held Jenna in silence.

"Dad, is Mary coming home for Christmas?" she asked.

I ran a hand through my hair. "No, I don't think so. Mary is very sick."

"Is she going to die?"

I wondered what that meant to my little girl.

"Yes, honey, I think she will die."

"If she is going to die, I want to give her my present first."

She ran over to the tree and lifted a small, inexpertly wrapped package. "I made her an angel." With excitement she unveiled a petite cardboard angel constructed with tape, glue, and paper clips.

"Dad, I think Mary likes angels."

I started to sob quietly. "Yeah, I think she likes angels, too."

In the silence of the lights we faced the death of a friend.

By the time I reached home it was well past midnight. Mary's brother had arrived from London and in deference I had left them alone to share the last few minutes together. Jenna had been put to bed and Keri, not knowing when I would return had sadly laid the Christmas packages under the tree. I sat down in the rocker in front of the illuminated Christmas tree and lay my head in my hands. Somewhere between the angel and Mary's house I had figured it out. The first gift of Christmas. It just came. It came to my heart. The first gift of Christmas was love. A parent's love. Pure as the first snows of Christmas. For God so loved his children that He sent His son, that we

might someday return to him. I understood what Mary had been trying to teach me. I stood up and walked up the stairs where my little girl lay sleeping. I picked up her warm little body and, cradling her tightly in my arms, brought her back down to the den. My tears fell on her hair. My little girl. My precious little girl. How foolish I'd been to let her childhood, her fleeting, precious childhood, slip away. Forever. In my young mind everything was so permanent and lasting. My little girl would be my little girl forever. But time would prove me wrong. Someday she'd grow up. Someday she'd be gone and I would be left with the memory of giggles and secrets I might have known.

Jenna took a deep breath and snuggled close for warmth. I held her little body tightly against mine. That was what it meant to be a father, to know that one day I would turn around and my little girl would be gone. To look upon the sleeping little girl and to die a little inside. For one precious, fleeting moment, to hold the child in my arms, and would that time stood still.

But none of that mattered now. Not now. Tonight Jenna was mine and no one could take this Christmas Eve away from me but me. How wise Mary had been. Mary, who knew the pain of a father sending his son away on that first Christmas morn, knowing full well the path that lay ahead. Mary understood Christmas. The tears in the Bible showed that. Mary loved with the pure, sweet love of a mother, a love so deep that it becomes an allegory for all other love. She knew that in my quest for success in this world I had been trading diamonds for stones. She knew, and she loved me enough to help me see. Mary had given me the greatest gift of Christmas. My daughter's childhood.

Some Say . . .

William Shakespeare

According to legend, Christmas was such a holy and magical time that malevolent spirits, ghosts, and witches were rendered powerless throughout the season. In Hamlet *(Act I, Scene I), Shakespeare's character Marcellus eloquently expresses this popular folk belief.*

from *Hamlet*, I:I

OME SAY that ever 'gainst that season comes

Wherein our Savior's birth is celebrated,

The bird of dawning singeth all night long:

And then, they say, no spirit dare stir abroad,

The nights are wholesome, then no planets strike,

No fairy takes nor witch hath power to charm,

So Hallow'd and so gracious is the time.

ALBERT CHEVALLIER TAYLER. *The Christmas Tree*. Private collection.
Photograph © The Bridgeman Art Library International Ltd., London/New York.

K.J. von Walla. *Children's Christmas*. Victoria & Albert Museum, London.
Photograph: Victoria & Albert Museum, London/Art Resource, N.Y.

The Gift Behind the Gift

GREGG EASTERBROOK

This essay appeared in The New York Times *on December 24, 1983, a contemplation on the true meaning of the excitement and anticipation of Christmas Eve, beyond the suspense of gifts waiting to be opened and the chance of a kiss under mistletoe.*

HE MOST SPLENDID Christmas gift, the most marveled and magic, is the gift that has not yet been opened. Opaque behind wrapping or winking foil, it is a box full of possibilities. An unopened present might be anything—gems, crystal, oranges, a promise of devotion. While the present is unopen, it can rest under the tree to be regarded and speculated upon at length, becoming whatever the recipient wishes.

Opening the present, by comparison, is often anticlimactic—no matter what the contents. For once opened, the gift passes from the enchanted realm of promise into the constrained reality of material possessions. Then it begins to impose terms on its owner—terms like sizes, warranties, colors, maintenance, accessories, storage space, assembly, extremely thick books with instructions. (Anyone receiving a personal computer this year should not expect to speak to loved ones again until next year.) Open a gift and, like the vacuum in a coffee can, the possibilities whoosh away, never to be recovered.

So it is that Christmas Eve is the best part of Christmas. Compared with the clamor and urgency of the day itself—the schedules to satisfy, the near-strangers to pretend to be close to, the post-gift frenzy to compare

windfalls—Christmas Eve is serene. It is the moment, still and expectant, when the warmth of the season may be felt for its own sake—the moment to light candles and listen for a sound in the distance. It is the moment when the meaning of the day, for those who wonder at it, may be contemplated without distraction from timetables or remote-controlled robots.

If anticipation is the essence of Christmas, Christmas Eve is the essence of anticipation. All the holiday's elves and henchmen revel in it. Snow is most beautiful while it falls, noiseless and free: Once on the ground, it succumbs to soot and stumbling tracks. The solitary country house is most beautiful observed from the cold hill above, as it shines out yellow squares of light and firesparks, promising friendship. The smell of Christmas cookies baking can be as satisfying as eating them, the first cup of Christmas cheer as gratifying as the next five combined. Lighting the tree is the finest part by far.

Often what precedes is better than what follows, even when, like Christmas Day, what follows is good. The first kiss, clumsy as it always is—first kisses generally have all the grace of two freight trains colliding on a dark siding—can be the most moving. However physically inadequate, it conveys the promise of further kisses, more esthetic or athletic, and the promise of proximity before and after, the companionship that a kiss seals. By that way of thinking, the most excitement available under the mistletoe is not the touch itself, but the instant just before, when she (or he, depending) steps forward to join you there. This is the moment when you know someone else wants to be near you, a moment blushing with what might be.

The original point of Christmas, now better reflected on tranquil Christmas Eve than on the madcap day itself, was to proclaim what might be. Wise men and shabby shepherds went to Bethlehem that first Christmas Eve

III

SONGS AND CELEBRATIONS

The First Nowell

In this traditional English carol, the word "nowell" or "noel" is repeated as a refrain, as a type of exclamation meaning "good news." This well-known carol dates from the seventeenth century.

HE FIRST NOWELL the angel did say
Was to certain poor shepherds in fields as they lay;
In fields where they lay keeping their sheep
On a cold winter's night that was so deep.
Nowell, Nowell, Nowell, Nowell,
Born is the King of Israel.

They looked up and saw a Star
Shining in the East, beyond them far
And to the earth it gave great light,
And so it continued both day and night.
Nowell, Nowell, Nowell, Nowell,
Born is the King of Israel.

This star drew nigh to the northwest
O'er Bethlehem it took its rest.
And there it did both stop and stay
Right over the place where Jesus lay.
Nowell, Nowell, Nowell, Nowell,
Born is the King of Israel.

Angels We
Have Heard on High

This traditional carol, also known as the "Westminster Carol," is believed to be a translation of a sixteenth-century French or Flemish antiphon-hymn, adapted from verses in alternating voices that are part of liturgical texts used in the Mass and at Vespers.

NGELS we have heard on high,

Sweetly singing o'er the plains;

And the mountains in reply

Echoing their joyous strains.

Refrain: *Gloria in excelsis Deo*

Gloria in excelsis Deo

Shepherds, why this jubilee?

Why your joyous songs prolong?

What the gladsome tidings be

Which inspire your heavenly song?

Refrain

Come to Bethlehem, and see

Him whose birth the angels sing;

Come adore on bended knee,

Christ, the Lord, our newborn King.

SEBASTIANO MAINARDI. *Nativity*. Pinacoteca, Vatican Museums, Vatican State.
Photograph: Scala/Art Resource, N.Y.

MELOZZA DA FORLI. *Music-making Angel*. Pinacoteca, Vatican Museums, Vatican State.
Photograph: Scala/Art Resource, N.Y.

ANGELS WE HAVE HEARD ON HIGH

Refrain

See Him in a manger laid
Whom the choir of angels praise
Mary, Joseph, lend your aid
While our hearts in love we raise

Refrain

It Came Upon
A Midnight Clear

Written in 1849 by Edmund H. Sears, a Unitarian minister in Weston, Massachusetts, the lyrics to this carol were set to music by Richard S. Willis, a journalist and editor in Detroit, Michigan, who was a friend of composer Felix Mendelssohn.

T CAME UPON a midnight clear,

That glorious song of old,

From angels bending near the earth

To touch their harps of gold;

Peace on the earth, good-will to men,

From heaven's all-gracious King;

The world in solemn stillness lay

To hear the angels sing.

Silent Night

"Silent Night" was composed in Oberndorf, Austria, one Christmas Eve in 1818 by Father Josef Mohr, a parish priest. He asked organist and schoolmaster Franz Gruber to set the words to music in time for the choir to sing the new song at Midnight Mass.

ILENT NIGHT, holy night.

All is calm, all is bright.

'Round yon Virgin Mother and Child.

Holy Infant so tender and mild,

Sleep in heavenly peace,

Sleep in heavenly peace.

Silent night, holy night,

Shepherds quake at the sight,

Glories stream from heaven afar,

Heav'nly hosts sing Alleluia;

Christ, the Saviour, is born,

Christ, the Saviour, is born!

Silent night, holy night,

Son of God, love's pure light

Radiant beams from thy holy face,

With the dawn of redeeming grace,

Jesus, Lord, at Thy birth,

Jesus, Lord, at Thy birth.

GERARD DAVID. *Holy Night*. c. 1495. Kunsthistoriches Museum, Gemaeldegalerie, Vienna.
Photograph: Erich Lessing/Art Resource, N.Y.

Joy to the World!

*The English hymnist and religious poet Isaac Watts (1674–1748) based the text of
this carol on Psalm 98. Lowell Mason of Medford, Massachusetts, later arranged the music from
sections of George Frederick Handel's "Messiah." The carol appeared in print in 1839.*

OY to the world! the Lord is come;

Let earth receive her King;

Let ev'ry heart prepare Him room,

And heav'n and nature sing,

And heav'n and nature sing,

And heav'n, and heav'n and nature sing.

Joy to the world! the Savior reigns;

Let men their songs employ;

While fields and floods, rocks, hills and plains,

Repeat the sounding joy,

Repeat the sounding joy,

Repeat, repeat the sounding joy.

He rules the world with truth and grace,

And makes the nations prove

The glories of His righteousness,

And wonders of His love,

And wonders of his love,

And wonders, and wonders of His love.

O Little Town of Bethlehem

Phillip Brooks, of Trinity Church in Boston, Massachusetts, wrote this after his visit to Bethlehem in 1865. Louis H. Redner, the church organist, wrote the melody. The carol was first sung by the children of the Holy Trinity Sunday School on Christmas Day, 1868.

 LITTLE TOWN
of Bethlehem,
How still we see thee lie!
Above thy deep and dreamless sleep
The silent stars go by;
Yet in thy dark streets shineth
The everlasting Light;
The hopes and fears of all the years
Are met in thee tonight.

For Christ is born of Mary,
And gathered all above,
While mortals sleep, the angels keep
Their watch of wondering love.
O morning stars, together
Proclaim the holy birth!
And praises sing to God the King,
And peace to men on earth.

O LITTLE TOWN OF BETHLEHEM

How silently, how silently
The wondrous gift is given!
So God imparts to human hearts
The blessings of His heaven.
No ear may hear His coming,
But in this world of sin,
Where meek souls will receive Him, still
The dear Christ enters in.

O holy Child of Bethlehem!
Descend to us, we pray;
Cast out our sin and enter in,
Be born in us today.
We hear the Christmas angels
The great glad tidings tell;
O come to us, abide with us,
Our Lord Emmanuel!

A Christmas Carol

GEORGE WITHER

*English poet and Puritan pamphleteer George Wither (1588–1667) was best known
for his songs and hymns. This poem, celebrating the feasting, revelry, and good will of the season,
was published in 1622, when Christmas was a carnival-like time of excesses.*

O NOW is come

        our joyful'st feast,

Let every man be jolly.

Each room with ivy leaves is drest,

And every post with holly.

Though some churls at our mirth repine,

Round your foreheads garlands twine,

Drown sorrow in a cup of wine,

And let us all be merry.

Now all our neighbors'

        chimneys smoke,

And Christmas blocks are burning;

Their ovens they with bak'd-meats choke,

And all their spits are turning.

Without the door let sorrow lie,

And if for cold it hap to die,

We'll bury 't in a Christmas pie,

And evermore be merry.

HENDRICK AVERCAMP. *A Scene on the Ice Near a Town*. The National Gallery, London.
Photograph © The National Gallery, London.

CHARLES GREEN. *"Christmas comes but once a year!"* Illustration from the Pears Christmas Annual, 1896.
Private collection. Photograph © The Bridgeman Art Library International Ltd., London/New York.

A CHRISTMAS CAROL

Now every lad is wondrous trim,

And no man minds his labor;

Our lasses have provided them

A bag-pipe and a tabor.

Young men and maids and girls and boys

Give life to one another's joys,

And you anon shall by their noise

Perceive that they are merry.

Rank misers now do sparing shun,

Their hall of music soundeth,

And dogs thence with whole shoulders run,

So all things there aboundeth.

The country folk themselves advance,

For crowdy-mutton's come out of France.

And Jack shall pipe and Jill shall dance,

And all the town be merry.

Ned Swash hath fetch'd his bands from pawn,

And all his best apparel;

Brisk Nell hath bought a ruff of lawn

With droppings of the barrel;

And those that hardly all the year

Had bread to eat or rags to wear,

Will have both clothes and dainty fare,

And all the day be merry.

Now poor men to the justices

With capons make their arrants,

And if they hap to fail of these

They plague them with their warrants.

But now they feed them with good cheer,

And what they want they take in beer,

For Christmas comes but once a year,

And then they shall be merry.

Good farmers in the country nurse

The poor, that else were undone.

Some landlords spend their money worse,

On lust and pride at London.

There the roisters they do play,

Drab and dice their land away,

Which may be ours another day;

And therefore let's be merry.

The client now his suit forbears,

The prisoner's heart is eased,

The debtor drinks away his cares,

And for the time is pleased.

Though others' purses be more fat,

Why should we pine or grieve at that?

Hang sorrow, care will kill a cat,

And therefore let's be merry.

Hark how the wags abroad do call

Each other forth to rambling;

Anon you'll see them in the hall

For nuts and apples scrambling.

Hark how the roofs with laughters sound!

Anon they'll think the house goes round,

For they the cellar's depth have found,

And there they will be merry.

The wenches with their wassail bowls

About the streets are singing,

The boys are come to catch the owls,

The wild mare in is bringing.

Our kitchen boy hath broke his box,

And to the dealing of the ox

Our honest neighbors come by flocks,

And here they will be merry.

Now kings and queens poor sheepcotes have,

And mate with everybody;

The honest now may play the knave,

And wise men play at noddy.

Some youths will now a-mumming go,

Some others play at rowlandhoe,

And twenty other gameboys moe,

Because they will be merry.

Then wherefore in these merry days

Should we, I pray, be duller?

No, let us sing some roundelays

To make our mirth the fuller.

And, whilst thus inspir'd we sing,

Let all the streets with echoes ring,

Woods and hills and everything,

Bear witness we are merry.

ANTONELLO DA MESSINA. *Madonna and Child*. c. 1475. National Gallery of Art, Washington, D.C.
Andrew W. Mellon Collection. Photograph © Board of Trustees, National Gallery of Art, Washington, D.C.

Do You Hear What I Hear?

Many carols have the Nativity as their central theme, describing the divine event with awe and emotion. In this simple, childlike carol, the good news of the birth of Christ is first told by the night wind to a small lamb, who then tells a shepherd, who tells a king.

 AID the night wind to the little lamb,
"Do you see what I see?
Way up in the sky, little lamb,
Do you see what I see?
A star, a star, dancing in the night
With a tail as big as a kite,
With a tail as big as a kite."

Said the little lamb to the shepherd boy,
"Do you hear what I hear?
Ringing through the sky, shepherd boy,
Do you hear what I hear?
A song, a song high above the trees
With a voice as big as the sea,
With a voice as big as the sea."

Said the shepherd boy to the mighty king,
"Do you know what I know?

In your palace warm, mighty king,

Do you know what I know?

A Child, a Child shivers in the cold—

Let us bring him silver and gold,

Let us bring him silver and gold."

Said the king to the people everywhere,

"Listen to what I say!

Pray for peace, people, everywhere,

Listen to what I say!

The Child, the Child sleeping in the night

He will bring us goodness and light,

He will bring us goodness and light."

Away in a Manger

Often ascribed to Martin Luther, this popular carol may have been inspired by one of Luther's hymns. The text of the poem, which appeared in print in Philadelphia in 1885, is likely of American origin. The poem has been set to forty-one different melodies.

WAY IN A MANGER no crib for a bed,
The little Lord Jesus laid down His sweet head,
The stars in the sky, looked down where He lay,
The little Lord Jesus, asleep on the hay.

The cattle are lowing, the poor baby wakes,
But little Lord Jesus, no crying He makes,
I love Thee, Lord Jesus, look down from the sky,
And stay by my cradle, till morning is nigh.

Be near me, Lord Jesus, I ask Thee to stay
Close by me forever, and love me, I pray;
Bless all the dear children in Thy tender care,
And take us to heaven to live with Thee there.

GIOVANNI DI PAOLA. *Nativity*. Mid to late 15th c.
Pinacoteca, Vatican Museums, Vatican State. Photograph: Scala/Art Resource, N.Y.

DOMENICO DI MICHELINO. *Adoration of the Magi.*
Pinacoteca, Vatican Museums, Vatican State. Photograph: Scala/Art Resource, N.Y.

Good King Wenceslas

This carol is based on the medieval legend of the miracle of St. Wenceslaus, Duke of Bohemia, which occurred on December 26, the feast of St. Stephen. The melody is a sixteenth-century liturgical song, with words written by John Mason Neale in 1866.

 OOD KING Wenceslas looked out,
On the Feast of Stephen,
When the snow lay round about,
Deep, and crisp, and even:
Brightly shone the moon that night,
Though the frost was cruel,
When a poor man came in sight,
Gath'ring winter fuel.

"Hither, page, and stand by me,
If thou know'st it, telling,
Yonder peasant, who is he?
Where and what his dwelling?"
"Sire, he lives a good league hence,
Underneath the mountain,
Right against the forest fence,
By Saint Agnes' fountain."

"Bring me flesh, and bring me wine,
Bring me pine logs hither:

Thou and I will see him dine,

When we bear them thither."

Page and monarch, forth they went,

Forth they went together;

Through the rude wind's wild lament

And the bitter weather.

"Sire, the night is darker now,

And the wind blows stronger;

Fails my heart, I know not how;

I can go no longer."

"Mark my footsteps, good my page;

Tread thou in them boldly:

Thou shalt find the winter's rage

Freeze thy blood less coldly."

In his master's step he trod,

Where the snow lay dinted;

Heat was in the very sod

Which the Saint had printed.

Therefore, Christian men, be sure,

Wealth or rank possessing,

Ye who now will bless the poor,

Shall yourselves find blessing.

The Holly and the Ivy

In early Europe, the holly was a symbol of the burning bush of Moses and the holiness of Mary. Its prickly points and berries were reminders that the Christ Child would one day wear a crown of thorns. Ivy was the symbol of Bacchus and, therefore, of human weakness.

HE HOLLY and the ivy,
When they are both full grown,
Of all the trees that are in the wood,
The holly tree bears the crown.
    Oh, the rising of the sun
    And the running of the deer,
    The playing of the merry organ,
    Sweet singing all in the choir.

The holly bears a blossom
As white as the lily flower,
And Mary bore sweet Jesus Christ
To be our sweet Saviour.
    Oh, the rising of the sun
    And the running of the deer,
    The playing of the merry organ,
    Sweet singing all in the choir.

The holly bears a berry
As red as any blood,

And Mary bore sweet Jesus Christ
To do poor sinners good.
    Oh, the rising of the sun
    And the running of the deer,
    The playing of the merry organ,
    Sweet singing all in the choir.

The holly bears a prickle
As sharp as any thorn,
And Mary bore sweet Jesus Christ
On Christmas Day in the morn.
    Oh, the rising of the sun
    And the running of the deer,
    The playing of the merry organ,
    Sweet singing all in the choir.

The holly and the ivy,
When they are both full grown,
Of all the trees that are in the wood
The holly tree bears the crown.
    Oh, the rising of the sun
    And the running of the deer,
    The playing of the merry organ,
    Sweet singing all in the choir.

WILLIAM-ADOLPHE BOUGUEREAU. *The Virgin and Angels*. Musée du Petite Palais, Paris.
Photograph: Giraudon/Art Resource, New York.

Hark! The Herald Angels Sing

The music for this carol was adapted in 1855 by William H. Cummings, the organist at Waltham Abbey in England, from Felix Mendelssohn's "Festgesang." The words had been written in 1739 by the minister Charles Wesley, a well-known writer of hymns and carols.

ARK! the herald angels sing,
"Glory to the newborn King!
Peace on earth, and mercy mild,
God and sinners reconciled."

Joyful, all ye nations rise,
Join the triumph of the skies;
With th'angelic host proclaim,
"Christ is born in Bethlehem."
Hark! the herald angels sing,
"Glory to the newborn King!"

Christ, by highest heav'n adored;
Christ, the everlasting Lord;
Late in time behold Him come,
Offspring of the favored one.
Veiled in flesh, the Godhead see;
Hail th'incarnate Deity

Pleased, as man with men to dwell,

Jesus, our Immanuel!

Hark! the herald angels sing,

"Glory to the newborn King!"

Hail! the heav'n-born Prince of Peace!

Hail! the Son of Righteousness!

Light and life to all He brings,

Ris'n with healing in His wings.

Mild He lays His glory by,

Born that man no more may die:

Born to raise the sons of earth,

Born to give them second birth.

Hark! the herald angels sing,

"Glory to the new-born King!"

O Come,
All Ye Faithful

*The words of this carol, also known as "Adestes Fideles," are from a Latin poem ascribed
to St. Bonaventure, a thirteenth-century Franciscan priest. The carol is often sung in the original
Latin. The music is attributed to John Francis Wade, an eighteenth-century music dealer.*

 COME, all ye faithful,

Joyful and triumphant,

O come ye, O come ye
   to Bethlehem!

Come and behold Him,

Born the King of Angels:

Refrain: O come, let us adore Him,

O come, let us adore Him,

O come, let us adore Him,

Christ the Lord.

Sing, choirs of angels,

Sing with exultation,

Sing all ye citizens of heav'n above:

Glory to God

In the highest;

Refrain

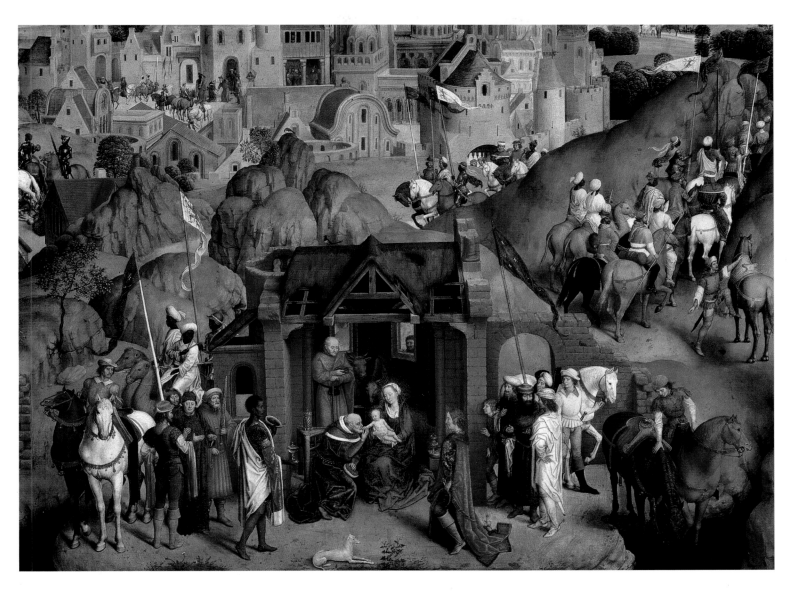

Hans Memling. *Adoration of the Magi*. Detail from *The Seven Joys of Mary*. 1480.
Alte Pinakothek, Munich. Photograph: Scala/Art Resource, N.Y.

SILVESTRO DEI GHERARDUCCI. *Nativity*. Single Leaf from a Gradual, Monastery of S. Maria degli Angeli, last third 14th c. Florence, Italy. M. 653, f. 1. The Pierpont Morgan Library, New York. Photograph: The Pierpont Morgan Library/Art Resource, N.Y.

Yea, Lord, we greet Thee,

Born this happy morning;

Jesus, to Thee be glory giv'n;

Word of the Father,

Now in flesh appearing;

Refrain

O Holy Night

*This French carol tells the story of the Holy Birth
as the world rejoices in the wonderment and expectation that
accompanied this blessed event.*

 Holy Night!
The stars are brightly shining,
It is the night of
    our dear savior's birth;

Long lay the world in
sin and error pining,
Till He appeared and the soul felt its worth.

A thrill of hope
the weary soul rejoices,
For yonder breaks
a new and glorious morn;
Fall on your knees,
Oh, hear the angel voices!
O night divine,
O night when Christ was born!
O night, O holy night, O night divine.

What Child is This?

WILLIAM CHATTERTON DIX

In 1865, William Chatterton Dix, an English poet, hymnist, and insurance company executive, wrote a poem entitled "The Manger Throne." In this well-loved carol, three of the poem's verses are set to the tune of "Greensleeves," a popular Elizabethan folk song.

HAT CHILD is this, Who, laid to rest, On Mary's
lap is sleeping?
Whom angels greet with anthems sweet, While
shepherds watch are keeping?
This, this is Christ the King, Whom shepherds guard and angels sing:
Haste, haste to bring Him laud, the Babe, the Son of Mary.

Why lies He in such mean estate Where ox and ass are feeding?
Good Christian, fear: for sinners here The silent Word is pleading.
This, this is Christ the King, Whom shepherds guard and angels sing:
This, this is Christ the King, the Babe, the Son of Mary.

So bring Him incense, gold and myrrh, Come, peasant, king to own Him;
The King of kings salvation brings, Let loving hearts enthrone him.
Raise, raise the Song on high, the Virgin sings her lullaby:
Joy, joy for Christ is born, the Babe, the Son of Mary.

IV

A CHILD'S CHRISTMAS

Yes, Virginia, There is a Santa Claus

Francis P. Church

Francis P. Church, The New York Sun's religious-affairs reporter, took on the task of answering a seemingly simple question, posed to him in a letter from an inquisitive little girl, and his eloquent response has provided an answer for children—and adults—for over a century.

Dear Editor:

I am 8 years old.

Some of my little friends say there is no Santa Claus.

Papa says, "If you see it in The Sun it's so. Please tell me the truth;

is there a Santa Claus?

—Virginia O'Hanlon

VIRGINIA, your little friends are wrong. They have been affected by the skepticism of a skeptical age. They do not believe except what they see. They think that nothing can be which is not comprehensible by their little minds. All minds, Virginia, whether they be men's or children's, are little. In this great universe of ours man is a mere insect, an ant, in his intellect, as compared with the boundless world about him, as measured by the intelligence capable of grasping the whole truth and knowledge.

Yes, Virginia, there is a Santa Claus. He exists as certainly as love and

generosity and devotion exist, and you know that they abound and give to your life its highest beauty and joy. Alas! how dreary would be the world if there were no Santa Claus. It would be as dreary as if there were no Virginias. There would be no childlike faith then, no poetry, no romance to make tolerable this existence. We should have no enjoyment, except in sense and sight. The eternal light with which childhood fills the world would be extinguished.

Not believe in Santa Claus! You might not as well believe in fairies! You might get your Papa to hire men to watch in all the chimneys on Christmas Eve to catch Santa Claus, but even if they did not see Santa Claus coming down, what would that prove? Nobody sees Santa Claus, but that is no sign that there is no Santa Claus. The most real things in the world are those that neither children nor men can see.

No Santa Claus! Thank God, he lives, and he lives forever. A thousand years from now, Virginia, nay, ten times ten thousand years from now, he will continue to make glad the heart of childhood.

The New York Sun, September 21, 1897

KARL ROGER. *Father Christmas.* Victoria & Albert Museum, London.
Photograph © The Bridgeman Art Library International Ltd., London/N.Y.

THOMAS NAST. *Merry Old Santa Claus.* 1880. The Granger Collection, New York.

Christmas in the Big Woods

from Little House in the Big Woods

LAURA INGALLS WILDER

Laura Ingalls Wilder's warm stories of simple, rugged pioneer life in the North Woods of Wisconsin at the end of the nineteenth century have become quintessential American classics. This Christmas morning resounds with good cheer.

CHRISTMAS was coming.

The little log house was almost buried in snow. Great drifts were banked against the walls and windows, and in the morning when Pa opened the door, there was a wall of snow as high as Laura's head. Pa took the shovel and shovelled it away, and then he shovelled a path to the barn, where the horses and the cows were snug and warm in their stalls.

The days were clear and bright. Laura and Mary stood on chairs by the window and looked out across the glittering snow at the glittering trees. Snow was piled all along their bare, dark branches, and it sparkled in the sunshine. Icicles hung from the eaves of the house to the snowbanks, great icicles as large at the top as Laura's arm. They were like glass and full of sharp lights.

Pa's breath hung in the air like smoke, when he came along the path from the barn. He breathed it out in clouds and it froze in white frost on his mustache and beard.

When he came in, stamping the snow from his boots, and caught Laura up in a bear's hug against his cold, big coat, his mustache was beaded with little drops of melting frost.

Every night he was busy, working on a bracket as a Christmas present for Ma. He hung it carefully against the log wall between the windows, and Ma stood her little china woman on the shelf.

The little china woman had a china bonnet on her head, and china curls hung against her china neck. Her china dress was laced across in front, and she wore a pale pink china apron and little gilt china shoes. She was beautiful, standing on the shelf with flowers and leaves and birds and moons carved all around her, and the large star at the very top.

Ma was busy all day long, cooking good things for Christmas. She baked salt-rising bread and rye'n'Injun bread, and Swedish crackers, and a huge pan of baked beans, with salt pork and molasses. She baked vinegar pies and dried-apple pies, and filled a big jar with cookies, and she let Laura and Mary lick the cake spoon.

One morning she boiled molasses and sugar together until they made a thick syrup, and Pa brought in two pans of clean, white snow from outdoors. Laura and Mary each had a pan, and Pa and Ma showed them how to pour the dark syrup in little streams on to the snow.

They made circles, and curlicues, and squiggledy things, and these hardened at once and were candy. Laura and Mary might eat one piece each, but the rest was saved for Christmas Day.

All this was done because Aunt Eliza and Uncle Peter and the cousins, Peter and Alice and Ella, were coming to spend Christmas.

The day before Christmas they came. Laura and Mary heard the gay

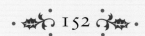

ringing of sleigh bells, growing louder every moment, and then the big bob-sled came out of the woods and drove up to the gate. Aunt Eliza and Uncle Peter and the cousins were in it, all covered up, under blankets and robes and buffalo skins.

They were wrapped up in so many coats and mufflers and veils and shawls that they looked like big, shapeless bundles.

When they all came in, the little house was full and running over. Black Susan ran out and hid in the barn, but Jack leaped in circles through the snow, barking as though he would never stop. Now there were cousins to play with!

As soon as Aunt Eliza had unwrapped them, Peter and Alice and Ella and Laura and Mary began to run and shout. At last Aunt Eliza told them to be quiet. Then Alice said: "I'll tell you what let's do. Let's make pictures."

Alice said they must go outdoors to do it, and Ma thought it was too cold for Laura to play outdoors. But when she saw how disappointed Laura was, she said she might go, after all, for a little while. She put on Laura's coat and mittens and the warm cape with the hood, and wrapped a muffler around her neck, and let her go.

Laura had never had so much fun. All morning she played outdoors in the snow with Alice and Ella and Peter and Mary, making pictures. The way they did it was this:

Each one by herself climbed up on a stump, and then all at once, hold-ing her arms out wide, they fell off the stumps into the soft, deep snow. They fell flat on their faces. Then they tried to get up without spoiling the marks they made when they fell. If they did it well, there in the snow were five

Robert Walter Weir. *St. Nicholas*. c. 1837. National Museum of American Art, Washington, D.C.
Photograph: National Museum of American Art, Washington, D.C./Art Resource, N.Y.

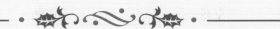

holes, shaped almost exactly like four little girls and a boy, arms and legs and all. They called these their pictures.

They played so hard all day that when night came they were too excited to sleep. But they must sleep, or Santa Claus would not come. So they hung their stockings by the fireplace, and said their prayers, and went to bed— Alice and Ella and Mary and Laura all in one big bed on the floor.

Peter had the trundle bed. Aunt Eliza and Uncle Peter were going to sleep in the big bed, and another bed was made on the attic floor for Pa and Ma. The buffalo robes and all the blankets had been brought in from Uncle Peter's sled, so there were enough covers for everybody.

In the morning they all woke up almost at the same moment. They looked at their stockings, and something was in them. Santa Claus had been there. Alice and Ella and Laura in their red flannel nightgowns and Peter in his red flannel nightshirt, all ran shouting to see what he had brought.

In each stocking there was a pair of bright red mittens, and there was a long, flat stick of red-and-white striped peppermint candy, all beautifully notched along each side.

They were all so happy they could hardly speak at first. They just looked with shining eyes at those lovely Christmas presents. But Laura was happiest of all. Laura had a rag doll.

She was a beautiful doll. She had a face of white cloth with black button eyes. A black pencil made her eyebrows, and her cheeks and her mouth were red with the ink made from pokeberries. Her hair was black yarn that had been knit and ravelled, so that it was curly.

She had little red flannel stockings and little black cloth gaiters for shoes, and her dress was pretty pink and blue calico.

She was so beautiful that Laura could not say a word. She just held her tight and forgot everything else. She did not know that every one was looking at her, till Aunt Eliza said:

"Did you ever see such big eyes!"

The other girls were not jealous because Laura had mittens, and candy, *and* a doll, because Laura was the littlest girl, except Baby Carrie and Aunt Eliza's little baby, Dolly Varden. The babies were too small for dolls. They were so small they did not even know about Santa Claus. They just put their fingers in their mouths and wriggled because of the excitement.

Laura sat down on the edge of the bed and held her doll. She loved her red mittens and she loved the candy, but she loved her doll best of all. She named her Charlotte.

Then they all looked at each other's mittens, and tried on their own, and Peter bit a large piece out of his stick of candy, but Alice and Ella and Mary and Laura licked theirs, to make it last longer.

"Well, well!" Uncle Peter said. "Isn't there even one stocking with nothing but a switch in it? My, my, have you all been such good children?"

But they didn't believe that Santa Claus could, really, have given any of them nothing but a switch. That happened to some children, but it couldn't happen to them. It was so hard to be good all the time, every day, for a whole year.

"You mustn't tease the children, Peter," Aunt Eliza said.

Ma said, "Laura, aren't you going to let the other girls hold your doll?" She meant, "Little girls must not be so selfish."

So Laura let Mary take the beautiful doll, and then Alice held her a minute, and then Ella. They smoothed the pretty dress and admired the red

flannel stockings and the gaiters, and the curly woolen hair. But Laura was glad when at last Charlotte was safe in her arms again.

Pa and Uncle Peter had each a pair of new, warm mittens, knit in little squares of red and white. Ma and Aunt Eliza had made them.

Aunt Eliza had brought Ma a large red apple stuck full of cloves. How good it smelled! And it would not spoil, for so many cloves would keep it sound and sweet.

Ma gave Aunt Eliza a little needle-book she had made, with bits of silk for covers and soft white flannel leaves into which to stick the needles. The flannel would keep the needles from rusting.

They all admired Ma's beautiful bracket, and Aunt Eliza said that Uncle Peter had made one for her—of course, with different carving.

Santa Claus had not given them anything at all. Santa Claus did not give grown people presents but that was not because they had not been good. Pa and Ma were good. It was because they were grown up, and grown people must give each other presents.

Then all the presents must be laid away for a little while. Peter went out with Pa and Uncle Peter to do the chores, and Alice and Ella helped Aunt Eliza make the beds, and Laura and Mary set the table, while Ma got breakfast.

The Boy Who Laughed at Santa Claus

OGDEN NASH

*Ogden Nash, born in 1902, was a master of modern light verse. He wrote for
The New Yorker for many years and published several books of poems. The fate of Jabez,
the boy who said there was no Santa Claus, was more than fitting.*

I N BALTIMORE there lived a boy.

He wasn't anybody's joy.

Although his name was Jabez Dawes,

His character was full of flaws.

In school he never led the classes,

He hid old ladies' reading glasses.

His mouth was open while he chewed,

And elbows to the table glued.

He stole the milk of hungry kittens,

And walked through doors marked No Admittance.

He said he acted thus because

There wasn't any Santa Claus.

Another trick that tickled Jabez

Was crying "Boo!" at little babies.

He brushed his teeth, they said in town,

Sideways instead of up and down.

Yet people pardoned every sin

Norman Rockwell. *The Discovery*. 1956.
Photograph courtesy The Norman Rockwell Museum at Stockbridge.

NORMAN ROCKWELL. *Santa Reading Mail*, *The Saturday Evening Post* cover, December 21, 1935. Photograph courtesy The Norman Rockwell Museum at Stockbridge.

And viewed his antics with a grin

Till they were told by Jabez Dawes,

"There isn't any Santa Claus!"

Deploring how he did behave,

His parents quickly sought their grave.

They hurried through the portals pearly,

And Jabez left the funeral early.

Like whooping cough, from child to child,

He sped to spread the rumor wild:

"Sure as my name is Jabez Dawes

There isn't any Santa Claus!"

Slunk like a weasel or a marten

Through nursery and kindergarten,

Whispering low to every tot,

"There isn't any, no, there's not!

No beard, no pipe, no scarlet clothes,

No twinkling eyes, no cherry nose,

No sleigh, and furthermore, by Jiminy,

Nobody's coming down the chimney!"

The children wept all Christmas Eve

And Jabez chortled up his sleeve.

No infant dared hang up his stocking

For fear of Jabez' ribald mocking.

He sprawled on his untidy bed,

Fresh malice dancing in his head,

When presently with scalp a-tingling,

Jabez heard a distant jingling;

He heard the crunch of sleigh and hoof

Crisply alighting on the roof.

What good to rise and bar the door?

A shower of soot was on the floor.

Jabez beheld, oh, awe of awes,

The fireplace full of Santa Claus!

Then Jabez fell upon his knees

With cries of "Don't," and "Pretty please."

He howled, "I don't know where you read it.

I swear some other fellow said it!"

"Jabez," replied the angry saint,

"It isn't I, it's you that ain't.

Although there—is—a Santa Claus,

There isn't any Jabez Dawes!"

Said Jabez then with impudent vim,

"Oh, yes there is; and I am him!

Your language don't scare me, it doesn't—"

And suddenly he found he wasn't!

From grinning feet to unkempt locks

Jabez became a jack-in-the-box,

An ugly toy in Santa's sack,

Mounting the flue on Santa's back.

The neighbors heard his mournful squeal;

They searched for him, but not with zeal.

No trace was found of Jabez Dawes,

Which led to thunderous applause,

And people drank a loving cup

And went and hung their stockings up.

All you who sneer at Santa Claus,

Beware the fate of Jabez Dawes,

The saucy boy who told the saint off;

The child who got him, licked his paint off.

Susie's Letter from Santa

MARK TWAIN

Samuel Langhorne Clemens (1835–1910) wrote under the pseudonym Mark Twain. As the creator of a legendary American boy, Huck Finn, he gained the love of readers everywhere, but he must have known well the heart of a little girl when he penned this glorious letter from Santa.

Christmas Morning

Y DEAR Susie Clemens:

I have received and read all the letters which you and your little sister have written me by the hand of your mother and your nurses; I have also read those which you little people have written me with your own hands—for although you did not use any characters that are in grown people's alphabet, you used the characters that all children in all lands on earth and in the twinkling stars use; and as all my subjects in the moon are children and use no characters but that, you will easily understand that I can read your and your baby sister's jagged and fantastic marks without any trouble at all. But I had trouble with those letters which you dictated through your mother and the nurses, for I am a foreigner and cannot read English writing well. You will find that I made no mistakes about the things which you and the baby ordered in your own letters—I went down your chimney at midnight when you were asleep and delivered them all myself—and kissed both of you, too, because you are good children, well trained, nice mannered, and about the most obedient little people I ever saw. But in the letter which you dictated there were some words which I could not make out for certain, and one or two small orders

NORMAN ROCKWELL. *Good Boys. The Saturday Evening Post* cover, December 4, 1926.
Photograph courtesy The Norman Rockwell Museum at Stockbridge.

I could not fill because we ran out of stock. Our last lot of kitchen furniture for dolls has just gone to a very poor little child in the North Star away up in the cold country above the Big Dipper. Your mama can show you that star and you will say: "Little Snow Flake" (for that is the child's name), "I'm glad you got that furniture, for you need it more than I." That is, you must *write* that, with your own hand, and Snow Flake will write you an answer. If you only spoke it she wouldn't hear you. Make your letter light and thin, for the distance is great and the postage very heavy.

There was a word or two in your mama's letter which I couldn't be certain of. I took it to be "a trunk full of doll's clothes." Is that it? I will call at your kitchen door about nine o'clock this morning to inquire. But I must not see anybody and I must not speak to anybody but you. When the kitchen doorbell rings, George must be blindfolded and sent to open the door. Then he must go back to the dining room or the china closet and take the cook with him. You must tell George he must walk on tiptoe and not speak—otherwise he will die someday. Then you must go up to the nursery and stand on a chair or the nurse's bed and put your ear to the speaking tube that leads down to the kitchen and when I whistle through it you must speak in the tube and say, "Welcome, Santa Claus!" Then I will ask whether it was a trunk you ordered or not. If you say it was, I shall ask you what *color* you want the trunk to be. Your mama will help you to name a nice color and then you must tell me every single thing in detail which you want the trunk to contain. Then when I say "Good-bye and a merry Christmas to my little Susie Clemens," you must say "Good-bye, good old Santa Claus, I thank you very much and please tell that little Snow Flake I will look at her star tonight and she must look down here—I will be right in the west bay window; and every

fine night I will look at her star and say, 'I know somebody up there and *like* her, too.'" Then you must go down into the library and make George close the doors that open into the main hall and everybody must keep still for a little while. Then while you are waiting I will go to the moon and get those things and in a few minutes I will come down the chimney that belongs to the fireplace in the hall—if it is a trunk you want—because I couldn't get such a large thing as a trunk down the nursery chimney, you know.

People may talk if they want, till they hear my footsteps in the hall. Then you may tell them to keep quiet a little while until I go up the chimney. Maybe you will not hear my footsteps at all—so you may go now and then and peep through the dining-room doors, and by and by you will see that which you want, right under the piano in the drawing room—for I shall put it there. If I should leave any snow in the hall, you must tell George to sweep it into the fireplace, for I haven't time to do such things. George must not use a broom, but a rag—or he will die someday. You watch George and don't let him run into danger. If my boot should leave a stain on the marble, George must not holystone it away. Leave it there always in memory of my visit; and whenever you look at it or show it to anybody you must let it remind you to be a good little girl. Whenever you are naughty and somebody points to that mark which your good old Santa Claus's boot made on the marble, what will you say, little sweetheart?

Good-bye for a few minutes, till I come down and ring the kitchen doorbell.

Your loving Santa Claus

Whom people sometimes call

"The Man in the Moon"

A Visit from St. Nicholas

CLEMENT CLARKE MOORE

Born in 1779, Clement Clarke Moore, scholar and Episcopal bishop of the diocese of New York, stepped out of character in 1822 to write these magical verses for his three children about what happened on the "night before Christmas."

'TWAS the night before Christmas,
when all through the house
Not a creature was stirring, not
even a mouse.
The stockings were hung by the chimney with care,
In hopes that St. Nicholas soon would be there.
The children were nestled all snug in their beds
While visions of sugarplums danced in their heads;
And mamma in her kerchief, and I in my cap
Had just settled our brains for a long winter's nap—
When out on the lawn there arose such a clatter
I sprang from my bed to see what was the matter.
Away to the window I flew like a flash,
Tore open the shutter, and threw up the sash.
The moon on the breast of the new-fallen snow
Gave a lustre of midday to objects below;
When what to my wondering eyes should appear
But a miniature sleigh and eight tiny reindeer,
With a little old driver, so lively and quick,

ARTHUR RACKHAM. Illustration from *The Night Before Christmas*,
by Clement Clarke Moore. 1931. Private collection.
Photograph © The Bridgeman Art Library International Ltd., London/New York.

DENLOW. *The Night Before Christmas*. 1903. Stapleton Collection.
Photograph © The Bridgeman Art Library International Ltd., London/New York.

A VISIT FROM ST. NICHOLAS

I knew in a moment it must be St. Nick!

More rapid than eagles his coursers they came,

And he whistled and shouted and called them by name.

"Now, Dasher! now, Dancer! now, Prancer and Vixen!

On, Comet! on, Cupid! on, Donder and Blitzen!—

To the top of the porch, to the top of the wall,

Now dash away, dash away, dash away all!"

As dry leaves that before the wild hurricane fly,

When they meet with an obstacle mount to the sky,

So, up to the housetop the coursers they flew,

With a sleigh full of toys—and St. Nicholas, too.

And then in a twinkling I heard on the roof

The prancing and pawing of each little hoof.

As I drew in my head and was turning around,

Down the chimney St. Nicholas came with a bound:

He was dressed all in fur from his head to his foot,

And his clothes were all tarnished with ashes and soot:

A bundle of toys he had flung on his back,

And he looked like a peddler just opening his pack.

His eyes, how they twinkled! his dimples, how merry!

His cheeks were like roses, his nose like a cherry;

His droll little mouth was drawn up like a bow,

And the beard on his chin was as white as the snow.

The stump of a pipe he held tight in his teeth

And the smoke, it encircled his head like a wreath.

He had a broad face and a little round belly

That shook, when he laughed, like a bowl full of jelly.

A VISIT FROM ST. NICHOLAS

He was chubby and plump—a right jolly old elf;

And I laughed, when I saw him, in spite of myself.

A wink of his eye, and a twist of his head

Soon gave me to know I had nothing to dread.

He spoke not a word, but went straight to his work,

And filled all the stockings; then turned with a jerk,

And laying his finger aside of his nose,

And giving a nod, up the chimeny he rose.

He sprang to his sleigh, to the team gave a whistle,

 And away they all flew, like the down of a thistle,

But I heard him exclam, ere he drove out of sight,

"Happy Christrnas to all, and to all a good night!"

FROM *The Father Christmas Letters*

J. R. R. TOLKIEN

For over twenty years the Tolkien children mysteriously received letters from the North Pole, from Father Christmas and his assistant, the mischievous North Polar Bear, and his secretary, the elf Ilbereth. The enchanting tales are favorites of adults and children alike.

1929

 T IS A LIGHT Christmas again, I am glad to say—the Northern Lights have been specially good. We had a bonfire this year (to please the Polar Bear), to celebrate the coming in of winter. The Snow-elves let off all the rockets together which surprised us both. I have tried to draw you a picture of it, but really there were hundreds of rockets. You can't see the Elves at all against the snow background. The bonfire made a hole in the ice and woke up the Great Seal, who happened to be underneath. The Polar Bear let off 20,000 silver sparklers afterwards—used up all my stock, so that is why I had none to send you. Then he went for a holiday!!!—to north Norway—and stayed with a wood-cutter called Olaf, and came back with his paw all bandaged just at the beginning of our busy times.

There seem more children than ever in all the countries I specially look after. It is a good thing clocks don't tell the same time all over the world or I should never get round, although when my magic is strongest—at Christmas—I can do about a thousand stockings a minute, if I have it all planned

out beforehand. You could hardly guess the enormous piles of lists I make out. I seldom get them mixed. But I am rather worried this year. You can guess from my pictures what happened. The first one shows you my office and packing room and the Polar Bear reading out names while I copy them down. We had awful gales here, worse than you did, tearing clouds of snow to a million tatters, screaming like demons, burying my house almost up to the roofs. Just at the worst the Polar Bear said it was stuffy! and opened a north window before I could stop him. Look at the result—only actually the North Polar Bear was buried in papers and lists; but that did not stop him laughing.

LAST LETTER

I am so glad you did not forget to write to me again this year. The number of children who keep up with me seems to be getting smaller. I expect it is because of this horrible war, and that when it is over things will improve again, and I shall be as busy as ever. But at present so terribly many people have lost their homes, or have left them; half the world seems in the wrong place! And even up here we have been having troubles. I don't mean only with my stores; of course they are getting low. They were already last year, and I have not been able to fill them up, so that I have now to send what I can, instead of what is asked for. But worse than that has happened.

I expect you remember that some years ago we had trouble with the Goblins, and we thought we had settled it. Well it broke out again this autumn, worse than it has been in centuries. We have had several *battles,* and for a while my house was besieged. In November it began to look likely that

it would be captured, and all my goods, and that Christmas stockings would remain empty all over the world. Would not that have been a calamity? It has not happened—and that is largely due to the efforts of Polar Bear—but it was not until the beginning of this month that I was able to send out any messengers! I expect the Goblins thought that with so much war going on this was a fine chance to recapture the North. They must have been preparing for some years; and they made a huge new tunnel which had an outlet many miles away. It was early in October that they suddenly came out in *thousands.* Polar Bear says there were at least a *million,* but that is his favourite big number. Anyway he was still fast asleep at the time, and I was rather drowsy myself.

The weather was rather warm for the time of the year, and Christmas seemed far away. There were only one or two Elves about the place; and of course Paksu and Valkotukka (also fast asleep). Luckily Goblins cannot help yelling and beating on drums when they mean to fight; so we all woke up in time, and got the gates and doors barred and the windows shuttered. Polar Bear got on the roof and fired rockets into the Goblin hosts as they poured up the long reindeer-drive; but that did not stop them for long. We were soon surrounded. I have not time to tell you all the story. I had to blow three blasts on the great Horn (Windbeam). It hangs over the fire-place in the hall, and if I have not told you about it before it is because I have not had to blow it for over four hundred years. Its sound carries as far as the North Wind blows. All the same, it was three whole days before help came: Snow-boys, Polar Bears, and hundreds and hundreds of Elves. They came up behind the Goblins; and Polar Bear (really awake this time) rushed out with a blazing branch off the fire in each paw. He must have killed dozens of Goblins (he

says a million). But there was a big battle down in the plain near the North Pole in November, in which the Goblins brought hundreds of new companies out of their tunnels. We were driven back to the Cliff, and it was not until Polar Bear and a party of his younger relatives crept out by night, and blew up the entrance to the new tunnels with nearly 100 lbs. of gunpowder, that we got the better of them— for the present. But bang went all the stuff for making fireworks and crackers (the cracking part) for some years. The North Pole cracked and fell over (for the second time) and we have not yet had time to mend it. Polar Bear is rather a hero (I hope he does not think so himself). But of course he is a very MAGICAL animal really, and Goblins can't do much to him, when he is awake and angry. I have seen their arrows bouncing off him and breaking.

Well, that will give you some idea of events, and you will understand why I have not had time to draw a picture this year—rather a pity, because there have been such exciting things to draw—and why I have not been able to collect the usual things for you, or even the very few you asked for . . .

I suppose after this year you will not be hanging your stocking any more. I shall have to say "goodbye," more or less: I mean, I shall not forget you. We always keep the names of our old friends, and their letters; and later on we hope to come back when they are grown up and have houses of their own and children.

The True Story of Santy Claus

JOHN MACY

John Macy's serious look at the development of the Santa Claus legend dismisses the image of the jolly old elf we think of as Santa Claus who bears no resemblance to the real St. Nicholas, son of a wealthy merchant from Asia Minor and the patron saint of giving.

F WE SHOULD WAKE on the sixth of December and find our stockings full of candy and toys we should think that the ruddy old fellow who comes down the chimney had lost his wits and arrived about three weeks too soon.

But his arrival would seem exactly on time to children in other parts of the world. For the feast of Saint Nicholas is the sixth of December, and how he became the patron saint of the day of the Saint of saints, the Christ child, is a story.

It is the story of a story. And when we say that it is true we shall remember that truth lives in the region of dreams. We shall be true to a glorious legend and to the way the legend has come down to us. Truth here consists in knowing that Santy Claus does come down the chimney and fill our stockings. If we do not believe that truth, we are lost souls and beauty and poetry, the only real truth, mean nothing.

Nicholas was an actual person. Though he is the most popular saint in the calendar, not excepting St. Christopher and St. Francis, we know little about the man to whom so many lovely deeds, human and miraculous, have been ascribed. He was bishop of Myra, in Lycia, Asia Minor, in the first part

of the fourth century of the Christian Era. Asia Minor is far away from reindeer and Santy Claus, but the world of faith and fable is small and ideas travel far if they have centuries of time for their journey round the world. And Asia Minor is the cradle of all Christian ideas.

From the day of his birth Nicholas revealed his piety and grace. He refused on fast days to take the natural nourishment of a child. He was the youngest bishop in the history of the church. He was persecuted and imprisoned with many other Christians during the reign of the Roman emperor Diocletian, and was released and honored when Constantine the Great established the Christian Church as the official religion, or at least recognized and encouraged it. Under Constantine, in 325, was held the first general council of the Christians at Nicaea, where many important matters were decided. These matters belong to theology and are not in our picture, but Nicholas may have had a hand, a vigorous hand, in them. One of the arguers who seemed to Nicholas, and to the later orthodox church, a dangerous heretic, so roused the righteous ire of the saint that Nicholas smote him in the jaw. This is one of the first episodes in militant Christianity.

About two hundred years after his death Nicholas was a great figure in Christian legend, and Justinian, the last powerful Roman emperor in the East, built a church in honor of St. Nicholas in Constantinople. But the bones of the saint were not allowed to rest in peace in his home town, Myra, where he was probably buried. About seven hundred years after his death, in the eleventh century, what remained of the earthly Nicholas was dug up and moved to the city of Bari, in Italy. In its day it was one of many important seaports that dominated Mediterranean traffic. The merchants of Bari organized a predatory expedition to the burial place of Nicholas, stole the bones, reburied them in Bari and built a church which was long an objective for

KARL ROGER. *Father Christmas with Children.* Victoria & Albert Museum, London.
Photograph © The Bridgeman Art Library International Ltd., London/N.Y.

NORMAN ROCKWELL. *Santa Asleep with Elves. The Saturday Evening Post* cover,
December 2, 1922. Photograph courtesy the Archives of the American Illustrators Gallery,
New York City. © 1998 ASaP of Holderness, NH.

religious pilgrims and is still worth the travel of a lover of art and architecture. The city of Venice, not to be outdone by a rival maritime town, also claims to enshrine the bones of the saint. So the curious tourist may take his choice. The bones are dust, wherever they lie. The churches in Bari and in many cities of Europe still stand; there are more than four hundred dedicated to Nicholas in England. More important, the spirit of the saint is alive throughout the Christian world.

Nicholas was not a barefoot recluse vowed to poverty. His father was a wealthy merchant, and his riches, inherited or created by the magic wand which fairy godfathers wield, enabled him to be a dispenser of the good things of life, an earthly representative of the Supreme Giver of gifts.

The most famous episode in his long career of benevolence is his rescue of the three dowerless maidens. An impoverished nobleman had three daughters whom he was about to send forth into a life of shame. Nicholas heard of the tragic situation and at night threw a purse of gold into the house. This furnished the dowry for the eldest daughter, and she was married.

After a little while, says the *Golden Legend*, which is the great medieval story of the saints, after a little while this holy hermit of God "threw in another mass of gold" and that provided a dowry for the second daughter. "And after a few days Nicholas doubled the mass of gold and cast it into the house." So the third daughter was endowed. The happy father, wishing to know his benefactor, ran after Nicholas and recognized him, but the holy man "required him not to tell nor discover this thing as long as he lived."

Thus Nicholas became not only the generous giver but the special patron saint of maidenhood and was so known and celebrated throughout the Middle Ages. Dante speaks in three short lines, as if he assumed that everybody already knew the story, of the generosity of Nicholas to maidens, "to lead their youth to honor." The Italian painters made much of this story. A fine pictorial representation of it is in the Metropolitan Art Museum in New York City. It is one of those dramatic paintings in which the old artists told a really moving tale long before the days of the camera and the moving picture. Inside the house you see the three distressed daughters and the still more dejected and ragged father. Outside is Nicholas climbing up at the door in the act of throwing the purse through a little window.

The story takes what seems an almost humorous turn. Let us imagine three purses or "masses" of gold. We recognize them, in conventional form, in the three gold balls over the pawnbroker's shop. Thus the holy man of the early Christian Church presides symbolically over a business which through-out Europe during the Middle Ages was conducted largely though not exclusively by members of the older Jewish Church. Pawnbroking included all forms of banking and moneylending with personal movable property as security. At first glance it does not seem quite appropriate that the charitable benevolent saint should become associated with a business, long notorious for exaction and usury, which the Mosaic law forbade and which the deriv-ative Christian morality condemned. One of the earliest acts of Christ was the expulsion of moneylenders from the temple; he "overthrew the tables of the money-changers" and scourged forth others who bought and sold.

But it may well be that the bankers and brokers wished to give sanctity and dignity to their business and so adopted the generous Nicholas as their heav-enly protector. Every profession, guild, trade, craft, had its favorite saint and was free to choose from the calendar; or, more likely, there was not much deliber-ate choice, these assimilations of legend to fact simply happened, nobody knows just how. Nicholas was adopted not only by the more or less respectable brokers but by thieves and pirates. The sinner as well as the honest man had his

NORMAN ROCKWELL. *Merrie Christmas—Colonial Couple Under Mistletoe.* 1928.
The Saturday Evening Post cover, December 8, 1928. Photograph courtesy the Archives of the
American Illustrators Gallery, New York City. © 1998 ASaP of Holderness, NH.

NORMAN ROCKWELL. *Christmas Trio.* 1923
Photograph courtesy The Norman Rockwell Museum at Stockbridge.

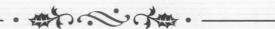

heavenly benefactor. And it is no more strange in the history of mythology that Nicholas should have been invoked by thieves than that the Greek-Roman god Mercury should have been the tutelary deity of robbers and tricksters.

Nicholas was the patron of all who went down to the sea in ships, whether bound on a predatory cruise or a military expedition or an errand of peaceful trade. The distinctions were not always clear in fact or theory. There are many stories of his having rescued sailors from shipwreck. It is written in the Roman Breviary, which is the "official account," that "in his youth on a sea voyage he saved the ship from a fearful storm." Greek and Russian sailors appeal to him for protection and carry in the cabin of the ships an image of the saint with a perpetually burning lamp. It is in accordance with the spirit of Christianity and other religions that a drowning man needs help, no matter what the moral purpose of his voyage through life may have been up to the hour of disaster.

Nicholas, however, was a dispenser of justice, according to the ideas of justice that prevailed when the stories about him grew up and took shape. One curious story of his judgment as patron of moneylending and trade reveals the attitude of those who made the story; it shows the somewhat confused relations between Jew and Gentile, relations familiarized for us by the story of Shylock. The tale is told in the *Golden Legend*, translated by Caxton, the father of English printing and a tireless interpreter of foreign books into our English tongue. I change a little Caxton's words, which are not quite modern in form and construction:

"There was a man who had borrowed of a Jew a sum of money and swore upon the altar of St. Nicholas that he would pay it back, as soon as he could, and gave no other pledge. The man kept the money so long that the Jew demanded payment. And the man said that he had paid. Then the Jew

summoned the debtor into court. The debtor brought a hollow staff in which he had put the money in gold. While he was taking oath he gave the staff to the Jew to hold. Then he swore that he had given the Jew more than he owed and asked the Jew to give him back the staff. The Jew, not suspecting the trickery, gave the staff back to the debtor, who took it and went away. Sleep overcame him and he lay down in the road. A cart ran over him and killed him and broke the staff so that the gold rolled out. When the Jew heard this he came and saw the fraud. Many people said to him that he should take the gold. But he refused saying that if the dead man were brought to life again by the power of St. Nicholas, he would take the money and become a Christian. So the dead man arose, and the Jew was christened."

Thus the ends of justice were served and everybody was happy.

The most important role of Nicholas to us at the present time is his patronage of schoolboys, for this brings him close to us as Santy Claus, the bearer of gifts and the special saint of childhood. He was himself the Boy Bishop. A famous story of him is that of his bringing to life three boys. On their way home, the tale runs, the boys stopped at a farmhouse. The farmer and his wife murdered them, cut their bodies in pieces and put them into casks used for pickling meat. St. Nicholas arrived, charged the murderers with their crime and caused the boys to rise from the casks fully restored. That is one reason, so far as there is any reason in fable, why schoolboys celebrated the feast of St. Nicholas on December sixth.

Intimately connected with the feast of Nicholas was the custom of electing a Boy Bishop for a limited number of days extending just over Christmas. To get something of the spirit of this ceremony and celebration we have only to think of a modern game played in New York and other American cities in which a boy is elected mayor for a day with a full staff of subordi-

nate juvenile officials. The motive of the modern custom is to teach youths civic virtue, public service and patriotism. The motive underlying the Boy Bishop was partly religious, partly childish love of pranks and parody, and partly a sort of democratic rebellion, tolerated for a short period each year, against constituted authority.

The Boy Bishop was dressed in handsome robes like a real bishop, and he and his companions led a mock solemn parade and in some cities actually took possession of the churches. There was much feasting, the way to a boy's heart being through his stomach as well as through gaudy garments; and there was on the part of elder participants a good deal of drinking. On the whole it was a charming and innocent affair. The boys took it seriously enough, especially the supper which concluded the performance. As early as the first part of the tenth century Conrad I, king of Germany, described a visit to a monastery when the revels were at their height. He was amused especially by the procession of the children, so grave and sedate that even when Conrad ordered his followers to throw apples down the aisle, the children did not lose their gravity. But these high jinks so near to sacred things met with opposition and censure. Ecclesiastical and civil authority shut down on the Boy Bishops and parades and ceremonies in one country after another. Grown people are not always profoundly wise about either the fooling or the intense seriousness of children. The Roman Catholic Church in the middle of the fifteenth century tried to suppress by edict the Boy Bishop and all the customs relating to him. In England, where this childish festival prevailed not only in the cathedral cities but in the small towns, the Protestant Reformation applied a depressing hand, and Queen Elizabeth, whose own court was gay with revelries, masques, interludes, finally abolished the Boy Bishop.

Childhood, however, has its revenges upon the interfering adult, with the

aid of the conniving adult who refuses to grow up. Nicholas remained the saint of children. In some countries his festival was taken over, assimilated to Christmas, partly because St. Nicholas Day is so near to Christmas and partly because in some parts of the world there arose a sort of Protestant hostility to the worship of saints. But custom and amusement prevail even when religion and history are forgotten or ignored. To cite another example as familiar as Christmas, on the evening of the last day of October children bob apples, make pumpkin jack-o'-lanterns, and play all kinds of tricks to pester innocent neighbors. They call the occasion Halloween, but few of them or their neighbors know that "hallow" means saint, and that the first of November is All Saints' Day.

So it is with Nicholas. He is honored and accepted with a kind of childish ignorance. Professor George H. McKnight of Ohio State University, who has given us the best account in English of the good St. Nicholas, begins his book by saying that strangely little is known of him in America. But he belongs to us by a very special inheritance. Our Dutch ancestors in New York—ancestry is a matter of tradition, not of blood—brought St. Nicholas over to New Amsterdam. The English colonists borrowed him from their Dutch neighbors. The Dutch form is San Nicolaas. If we say that rather fast with a stress on the broad double-A of the last syllable, a D or a T slips in after the N and we get "Sandyclaus" or "Santy Claus." And our American children are probably the only ones in the world who say it just that way; indeed the learned, and very British, *Encyclopaedia Britannica* calls our familiar form "an American corruption" of the Dutch. I suspect, however, that we should hear something very like it from the lips of children in Holland and Germany; in parts of southern Germany the word in sound, and I think in spelling, is "Santiklos."

However that may be, America owes the cheery saint of Christmas to Holland and Germany. In Belgium and Holland the festival of the saint is still

Child Whispering to Father Christmas. Victorian Christmas card. Private collection.
Photograph © The Bridgeman Art Library International Ltd., London/New York.

ETHEL PARKINSON. *Mother and Three Children.* Early 20th c., Faulkner & Co., Ltd., London.
Photograph © The Bridgeman Art Library International Ltd., London/New York.

observed on his birthday, December sixth, and the jollities and excitements are much the same as those that we enjoy at Christmas, with some charming local variations. Saint Nicholas is not the merry fellow with a chubby face and twinkling eye, but retains the gravity appropriate to a venerable bishop. He rides a horse or an ass instead of driving a team of reindeer. He leaves his gifts in stocking, shoes or baskets. And for children who have been very naughty, and whose parents cannot give him a good account of them, he leaves a rod by way of admonition, for he is a highly moral saint, though kind and forgiving. If the parents are too poor to buy gifts, the children say ruefully that the saint's horse has glass legs and has fallen down and broken his foot. The horse or ass of St. Nicholas is not forgotten; the children leave a wisp of hay for him, and in the morning it is gone.

As with us, the older people have their own festivities, suppers, exchange of gifts, surprises. But also as with our Christmas, the feast of Nicholas is primarily a day for children.

Where did Santy Claus get his reindeer? And how did the grave saint become that gnomelike fat fellow, with nothing ecclesiastic about him, so vividly described in Clement Moore's famous poem "'Twas the night before Christmas"? The answers to these questions are only provisional, matters of conjecture.

Notice that in Moore's poem, the form Santy Claus does not appear. The title of the poem is "A Visit from St. Nicholas," and in the verses the visitor is St. Nicholas, and "Saint Nick." The verses were written in the first half of the last century. The author was a distinguished Biblical scholar and professor in the General Theological Seminary in New York. In these verses he was writing not as a scholar but as a jolly human being, the father of a family taking a day off from his serious studies. His verses must represent the idea of Santy Claus that prevailed in his time, and long before his time in New York and far outside

New York, for they spread all over the country, are still reprinted every year.

Now in this delightful jingling poem there is not a touch of religion. The "jolly old elf" has not the slightest resemblance to a reverend saint. And there is no suggestion, except in the word Christmas, of any connection in thought or spirit with what is, excepting possibly Easter, the most sacred day in the whole Christian year. And similarly we may observe in our time many a gay Christmas party run its course without any of the participants giving a thought to a birth in a manger from which our year is dated. So Santy Claus is strangely different from his pious namesake and also in some places and among some people estranged from the very religious occasion to which he is attached!

But in some parts of America where the people are of Dutch or German descent there is a charming alliance between Santy Claus and the Christ child. It came about in this way: In some parts of Germany after the feast of St. Nicholas had been moved forward and identified with Christmas it was felt that the real patron of the day, the true giver of gifts, should be Christ Himself. This feeling probably arose from the Protestant objection to the worship of saints. So St. Nicholas was deposed from power; gradually, not by any sudden revolution, he disappeared in some places, from the customs long associated with him. But the customs remained. On Christmas Eve there were gifts of sweets and toys for good children. Or they put bowls in the window, and behold, in the morning they found that the windowpane had been taken out during the night and gifts laid in the bowls. The bringer of these gifts was not St. Nicholas but the Christ child, in popular German, Kriss Kringle. But among the German people in America the legend of Santy Claus still survived, and so Kriss Kringle is a combination of Santy Claus and the Christ child.

This combination gives us an inkling of what happened in the whole story of Christmas from earliest times. Santy Claus, the merry elf, is not Christian at

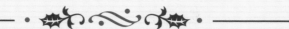

all, but pagan, coming down from times earlier than the Christian Era or at least earlier than the times when the Teutonic people were Christianized. He belongs to popular fairyland, the land of elves, gnomes, sprites, hobgoblins. In countless fairy tales there are good spirits and evil spirits. The evil spirits haunt the woods and molest innocent people. The good spirits aid the poor, bring gifts in the night, rescue princes in distress and so on.

These stories are not originally of Christian origin. They may not be definitely part of any of the religions which Christianity supplanted. Associated with them are popular festivals and ceremonies. It may well be that the apples in our Christmas stockings are the descendants of apples that grew on very old trees, trees older than history; perhaps there was a late harvest festival, or a kind of pagan Thanksgiving, presided over by a beneficent elf, and accompanied by dancing and feasting. We do not know.

But we do know that as Christianity developed, the Church encouraged all the popular customs, or may of them, took them over and associated them with Christian holidays. This may have been a deliberate attempt of the priests to win the favor of the people and make the new religion really popular, or the people may have made the transfer themselves by the vague and untraceable but very real process of folk poetry.

Now where did Santy Claus get his reindeer? There are not reindeer in Germany and probably never were, certainly not the kind that are broken to harness like horses. And oddly enough the reindeer does not appear in any of the surviving Christmas legends and customs in old Germany. The reindeer first paws the roofs of American houses. But of course he cannot be an American animal. The explanation, one explanation, is this:

There are reindeer in northern Scandinavia where they have been domesticated from time immemorial. Scandinavian and German legend and mythology

are closely related. The old German gods came from the north and many German folk tales are of Scandinavian origin. The reindeer of our Santy Claus certainly came from Lapland, and Santy is an arctic explorer, exploring the other way! Dr. Moore, with true poetic imagination, describes him as "dressed all in fur, from his head to his foot"—not in the red flannel with which we are accustomed to clothe him. Among the Germans or Dutch who came to this country there must have been a legend of a Scandinavian Santy, and in Germany the reindeer inexplicably got lost. Perhaps their bones will be found in a German forest by one of the literary archaeologists who dig into such matters. But no, the bones will never be found, for the reindeer are still alive and fly over the housetops.

The career of Santy Claus through the ages is as mysterious as his annual flight. One might suppose that he would have gone directly from Germany or Holland to their near neighbor England, as the Christmas tree was transplanted to England after the shortest possible journey. But there is every likelihood that Santy Claus, having become a good American colonist, recrossed the Atlantic in an English ship—or perhaps as the first transatlantic flier. He has long been a well-established figure in the Christmas customs not only of the mother country but in all parts of the British Empire. The allegiance of English children, however, is divided. Some believe that Santy Claus brings them their presents. Others believe in Father Christmas, a more recent creation, whom English artists represent as an old gentleman in what seems to be a sort of eighteenth-century costume with gaitered legs, a tail coat and a squarish beaver hat.

It is rather strange that English Christmas customs are not more closely imitated by American. We know nothing of the yule log, even in houses that have open fireplaces. Perhaps the reason that we borrowed little from the English Christmas is that the English who came to America, especially to New England, were not of the merrymaking kind; they would have

abhorred the idea of making Christmas an occasion for mirth and happiness. They would have groaned at one pretty custom, which is inherited directly from England and which their less godly descendants indulge in on Beacon Hill in Boston—the singing of carols in the streets on Christmas Eve. In all New England literature of the classical period there is scarcely a reference in prose or verse to Christmas, and that was the time when Dickens and Thackeray and other English writers, eagerly read in America, were giving the holiday new spirit and brightness in England.

Customs differ in different countries. A Russian coming from the country of which Nicholas is the chief saint would not at first sight understand our Santy Claus. He would see no relation between his saint before whose icon he bows and the figure in a red suit with a long white beard standing in front of a department store and doing his bit to keep a spirit of good cheer in that enormous American institution—Christmas trade. An American tourist brought up as a Protestant finding himself in an Italian city would look up in his guidebook an ornate Italian painting of St. Nicholas miraculously answering a prayer for help, and that tourist unless he had historical imagination might not realize that connection between this beautiful painting, the angel on his last Christmas tree at home and the letter that he wrote as a boy asking Santy Claus to bring him a new sled.

Yet these connections do exist, and they are very important, for they are bonds that hold the world together and help to give its disparate parts and antagonistic faiths a human unification. No other saint and few other men embrace such a wide variety of benevolent ideas as Nicholas, with such duration in time and such extent throughout the Christian world. And he is probably the only serious figure in religious history in any way associated with humor, with the spirit of fun. For he is the patron of giving. And it is fun to give.

V

O TANNENBAUM—
HOME FOR
THE HOLIDAYS

O Christmas Tree

The symmetry and perpetual green of the Christmas tree reflect the beauty and order of nature. Legend has it that the first American Christmas tree was seen in 1835 in the Massachusetts home of Charles Follen, a German immigrant and professor at Harvard.

 CHRISTMAS TREE!

O Christmas tree!

Your leaves are faithful ever!

O Christmas tree! O Christmas tree!

Your leaves are faithful ever!

Not only green when summer glows,

But in the winter when it snows,

O Christmas tree! O Christmas tree!

Your leaves are faithful ever!

O Christmas tree! O Christmas tree!

You are the tree most lovèd!

O Christmas tree! O Christmas tree!

You are the tree most lovèd!

How oft you've given me delight

When Christmas fires were burning bright!

O Christmas tree! O Christmas tree!

You are the tree most lovèd!

O Christmas tree! O Christmas tree!

Your faithful leaves will teach me

O CHRISTMAS TREE

O Christmas tree! O Christmas tree!
Your faithful leaves will teach me
That hope and love and constancy
Give joy and peace eternally.
O Christmas tree! O Christmas tree!
Your faithful leaves will teach me.

ANDY WARHOL. *Untitled (Christmas Tree Design)*. c. 1957.
© The Andy Warhol Foundation for the Visual Arts/ARS, N.Y.
Photograph: The Andy Warhol Foundation, Inc./Art Resource, N.Y.

FROM *The Fir Tree*

HANS CHRISTIAN ANDERSEN

*Hans Christian Andersen (1805–1875), the beloved storyteller from Denmark,
produced a well-known collection of fairy tales of mythical importance. In this tale a
storytelling tree discovers the importance of appreciating the present.*

"REJOICE in our presence!" said the Air and Sunlight;
"rejoice in thy own fresh youth!"

But the Tree did not rejoice at all; he grew and grew, and
was green both winter and summer. People that saw him
said, "What a fine tree!" and toward Christmas he was one of the first that
was cut down. The axe struck deep into the very pith; the Tree fell to the
earth with a sigh: he felt a pang—it was like a swoon; he could not think of
happiness, for he was sorrowful at being separated from his home, from the
place where he had sprung up. He knew well that he should never see his
dear old comrades, the little bushes and flowers around him, any more; perhaps not even the birds! The departure was not at all agreeable.

The Tree came to himself when he was unloaded in a courtyard with the
other trees, and heard a man say, "That one is splendid! we don't want the
others." Then two servants came in rich livery and carried the Fir tree into
a large and splendid drawing-room. Portraits were hanging on the walls, and
near the white porcelain stove stood two large Chinese vases with lions on
the covers. There, too, were large easy chairs, silken sofas, large tables full of
picture-books, and full of toys worth hundreds and hundreds of crowns—at
least the children said so. And the Fir tree was stuck upright in a cask that

was filled with sand: but no one could see that it was a cask, for green cloth was hung all around it, and it stood on a large gayly colored carpet. Oh, how the Tree quivered! What was to happen? The servants, as well as the young ladies, decorated it. On one branch there hung little nets cut out of colored paper, and each net was filled with sugar-plums; and among the other boughs gilded apples and walnuts were suspended, looking as though they had grown there, and little blue and white tapers were placed among the leaves. Dolls that looked for all the world like men—the Tree had never beheld such before—were seen among the foliage, and at the very top a large star of gold tinsel was fixed. It was really splendid—beyond description splendid.

"This evening!" said they all; "how it will shine this evening!"

"Oh," thought the Tree, "if the evening were but come! If the tapers were but lighted! And then I wonder what will happen! Perhaps the other trees from the forest will come to look at me! Perhaps the Sparrows will beat against the window-panes! I wonder if I shall take root here, and winter and summer stand covered with ornaments!"

He knew very much about the matter! but he was so impatient that for sheer longing he got a pain in his back, and this with trees is the same thing as a headache in us.

The candles were now lighted. What brightness! What splendor! The Tree trembled so in every bough that one of the tapers set fire to the foliage. It blazed up splendidly.

"Help! Help!" cried the young ladies, and they quickly put out the fire.

Now the Tree did not even dare tremble. What a state he was in! He was so uneasy lest he should lose something of his splendor, that he was quite bewildered amidst the glare and brightness; when suddenly both folding-

Illustration for *The Christmas Tree*, song written by J.E. Carpenter
and Henry Farmer. British Library, London.
Photograph © The Bridgeman Art Library International Ltd., London/New York.

doors opened, and a troop of children rushed in as if they would upset the Tree. The older persons followed quietly; the little ones stood quite still. But it was only for a moment; then they shouted so that the whole place reechoed with their rejoicing; they danced around the Tree, and one present after the other was pulled off.

"What are they about?" thought the Tree. "What is to happen now?" And the lights burned down to the very branches, and as they burned down they were put out, one after the other, and then the children had permission to plunder the Tree. So they fell upon it with such violence that all its branches cracked; if it had not been fixed firmly in the cask, it would certainly have tumbled down.

The children danced about with their beautiful playthings: no one looked at the Tree except the old nurse, who peeped between the branches but it was only to see if there was a fig or an apple left that had been forgotten.

"A story! a story!" cried the children, drawing a little fat man toward the Tree. He seated himself under it, and said: "Now we are in the shade, and the Tree can listen, too. But I shall tell only one story. Now which will you have: that about Ivedy-Avedy, or about Klumpy-Dumpy who tumbled downstairs, and yet after all came to the throne and married the princess?"

"Ivedy-Avedy!" cried some; "Klumpy-Dumpy!" cried the others. There was such a bawling and screaming—the Fir tree alone was silent, and he thought to himself, "Am I not to bawl with the rest?—am I to do nothing whatever?" for he was one of the company, and had done what he had to do.

And the man told about Klumpy-Dumpy that tumbled down, who notwithstanding came to the throne, and at last married the princess. And the children clapped their hands, and cried out, "Oh, go on! Do go on!" They

wanted to hear about Ivedy-Avedy, too, but the little man only told them about Klumpy-Dumpy. The Fir tree stood quite still and absorbed in thought; the birds in the woods had never related the like of this. "Klumpy-Dumpy fell downstairs, and yet he married the princess! Yes! Yes! That's the way of the world!" thought the Fir tree, and believed it all, because the man who told the story was so good-looking. "Well, well! who knows, perhaps I may fall downstairs, too, and get a princess as a wife!" And he looked forward with joy to the morrow, when he hoped to be decked out again with lights, playthings, fruits, and tinsel.

"I won't tremble tomorrow," thought the Fir tree. "I will enjoy to the full all my splendor. Tomorrow I shall hear again the story of Klumpy-Dumpy, and perhaps that of Ivedy-Avedy, too." And the whole night the Tree stood still and in deep thought.

In the morning the servant and the housemaid came in.

"Now, then, the splendor will begin again," thought the Fir. But they dragged him out of the room, and up the stairs into the loft; and here in a dark corner, where no daylight could enter, they left him. "What's the meaning of this?" thought the Tree. "What am I to do here? What shall I hear now, I wonder?" And he leaned against the wall, lost in reverie. Time enough had he, too, for his reflections; for days and nights passed on, and nobody came up; and when at last somebody did come, it was only to put some great trunks in a corner out of the way. There stood the Tree quite hidden; it seemed as if he had been entirely forgotten.

"'Tis now winter out of doors!" thought the Tree. "The earth is hard and covered with snow; men cannot plant me now, and therefore I have been put up here under shelter till the springtime comes! How thoughtful that is!

How kind man is, after all! If it only were not so dark here, and so terribly lonely! Not even a hare. And out in the woods it was so pleasant, when the snow was on the ground, and the hare leaped by; yes—even when he jumped over me; but I did not like it then. It is really terribly lonely here!"

"Squeak! squeak!" said a little Mouse at the same moment, peeping out of his hole. And then another little one came. They sniffed about the Fir tree, and rustled among the branches.

"It is dreadfully cold," said the Mouse. "But for that, it would be delightful here, old Fir, wouldn't it?"

"I am by no means old," said the Fir tree. "There's many a one considerably older than I am."

"Where do you come from," asked the Mice; "and what can you do?" They were so extremely curious. "Tell us about the most beautiful spot on the earth. Have you never been there? Were you never in the larder, where cheeses lie on the shelves, and hams hang from above; where one dances about on tallow-candles; that place where one enters lean, and comes out again fat and portly?"

"I know no such place," said the Tree, "but I know the woods, where the sun shines, and where the little birds sing." And then he told them all about his youth; and the little Mice had never heard the like before; and they listened and said:

"Well, to be sure! How much you have seen! How happy you must have been!"

"I?" said the Fir tree, thinking over what he had himself related. "Yes, in reality those were happy times." And then he told about Christmas Eve, when he was decked out with cakes and candles.

"Oh," said the little Mice, "how fortunate you have been, old Fir tree!"

"I am by no means old," said he. "I came from the woods this winter; I am in my prime, and am only rather short for my age."

"What delightful stories you know!" said the Mice: and the next night they came with four other little Mice, who were to hear what the tree recounted; and the more he related, the more plainly he remembered all himself; and it appeared as if those times had really been happy times. "But they may still come—they may still come. Klumpy-Dumpy fell downstairs and yet he got a princess," and he thought at the moment of a nice little Birch tree growing out in the woods; to the Fir, that would be a real charming princess.

"Who is Klumpy-Dumpy?" asked the Mice. So then the Fir tree told the whole fairy tale, for he could remember every single word of it; and the little Mice jumped for joy up to the very top of the Tree. Next night two more Mice came, and on Sunday two Rats, even; but they said the stories were not interesting, which vexed the little Mice; and they, too, now began to think them not so very amusing either.

"Do you know only one story?" asked the Rats.

"Only that one," answered the Tree. "I heard it on my happiest evening; but I did not then know how happy I was."

"It is a very stupid story. Don't you know one about bacon and tallow candles? Can't you tell any larder stories?"

"No," said the Tree.

"Then good-bye," said the Rats; and they went home.

At last the little Mice stayed away also; and the Tree sighed: "After all, it was very pleasant when the sleek little Mice sat around me and listened to

CLAUDE MONET. *Snow at Argenteuil*. c. 1874 Bequest of Anna Perkins Rogers.
Courtesy Museum of Fine Arts, Boston.

VIGGO JOHANSEN. *Happy Christmas*. Hirschsprungske Samling, Copenhagen.
Photograph © The Bridgeman Art Library International Ltd., London/New York.

what I told them. Now that too is over. But I will take good care to enjoy myself when I am brought out again."

But when was that to be? Why, one morning there came a quantity of people and set to work in the loft. The trunks were moved, the Tree was pulled out and thrown—rather hard, it is true—down on the floor, but a man drew him toward the stairs, where the daylight shone.

"Now a merry life will begin again," thought the Tree. He felt the fresh air, the first sunbeam—and now he was out in the courtyard. All passed so quickly, there was so much going on around him, that the Tree quite forgot to look to himself. The court adjoined a garden, and all was in flower; the roses hung so fresh and odorous over the balustrade, the lindens were in blossom, the Swallows flew by, and said, "Quirre-vit! my husband is come!" but it was not the Fir tree that they meant.

"Now, then, I shall really enjoy life," said he, exultingly, and spread out his branches; but, alas! they were all withered and yellow. It was in a corner that he lay, among weeds and nettles. The golden sat of tinsel was still on the top of the Tree, and glittered in the sunshine.

In the courtyard some of the merry children were playing who had danced at Christmas round the Fir tree, and were so glad at the sight of him. One of the youngest ran and tore off the golden star.

"Only look what is still on the ugly old Christmas tree!" said he, trampling on the branches, so that they all cracked beneath his feet.

And the Tree beheld all the beauty of the flowers, and the freshness in the garden; he beheld himself, and wished he had remained in his dark corner in the loft; he thought of his first youth in the woods, of the merry

Christmas Eve, and of the little Mice who had listened with so much pleasure to the story of Klumpy-Dumpy.

"Tis over—tis past!" said the poor Tree. "Had I but rejoiced when I had reason to do so! But now tis past, tis past!"

And the gardener's boy chopped the Tree into small pieces; there was a whole heap lying there. The wood flamed up splendidly under the large brewing copper, and it sighed so deeply! Each sigh was like a shot.

The boys played about in the court, and the youngest wore the gold star on his breast which the Tree had had on the happiest evening of his life. However, that was over now—the Tree was gone, the story at an end. All, all was over; every tale must end at last.

little tree

E. E. CUMMINGS

Self-described as "an author of pictures, a draughtsman of words,"
E. E. Cummings recalls the trimming of the Christmas tree in this delightful and tender poem.

ittle tree
little silent christmas tree
you are so little
you are more like a flower

who found you in the green forest
and were you very sorry to come away?
see   i will comfort you
because you smell so sweetly

i will kiss your cool bark
and hug you safe and tight
just as your mother would,
only don't be afraid

look   the spangles
that sleep all the year in a dark box
dreaming of being taken out and allowed to shine,
the balls the chains red and gold the fluffy threads,

little tree

put up your little arms
and i'll give them all to you to hold
every finger shall have its ring
and there won't be a single place dark or unhappy

then when you're quite dressed
you'll stand in the window for everyone to see
and how they'll stare!
oh but you'll be very proud

and my little sister and i will take hands
and looking up at our beautiful tree
we'll dance and sing
"Noel Noel"

Christmas at Bracebridge Hall

from The Sketch Book of Geoffrey Crayon

WASHINGTON IRVING

New York-born author Washington Irving (1783–1859) wrote the first literary description of Saint Nicholas to appear in America. His Christmas writings played an important part in reviving the old-fashioned celebrations and sentiments of the holiday.

HE DINNER was served up in the great hall, where the squire always held his Christmas banquet. A blazing crackling fire of logs had been heaped on to warm the spacious apartment, and the flame went sparkling and wreathing up the wide-mouthed chimney. . . .

We were ushered into this banquetting scene with the sound of minstrelsy; the old harper being seated on a stool beside the fireplace, and twanging the roast beef of old England, with a vast deal more power than melody. Never did Christmas board display a more goodly and gracious assemblage of countenances; those who were not handsome were, at least, happy; and happiness is a rare improver of your hard-favoured visage. The parson said grace, which was not a short familiar one, such as is commonly addressed to the deity, in these unceremonious days; but a long, courtly, well-worded one, of the ancient school. There was now a pause, as if something was expected, when suddenly the Butler entered the hall, with some degree of bustle; he

was attended by a servant on each side with a large wax light, and bore a silver dish, on which was an enormous pig's head, decorated with rosemary, with a lemon in its mouth, which was placed with great formality at the head of the table. The moment this pageant made its appearance, the harper struck up a flourish; at the conclusion of which the young Oxonian, on receiving a hint from the squire, gave, with an air of the most comic gravity, an old carol, the first verse of which was as follows:

> *Caput apri defero*
> *Reddens Laudes Domino.*
> The boar's head in hand bring I,
> With garlands gay and rosemary.
> I pray you all synge merily,
> *Qui estis in convivio. . . .*

When the cloth was removed, the butler brought in a huge silver vessel of rare and curious workmanship, which he placed before the squire. . . . The old gentleman's whole countenance beamed with a serene look of indwelling delight, as he stirred this mighty bowl. Having raised it to his lips, with a hearty wish of a merry Christmas to all present, he sent it brimming round the board, for every one to follow his example according to the primitive custom; pronouncing it "the ancient fountain of good fellowship, where all hearts met together." . . .

After the dinner table was removed, the hall was given up to the younger members of the family, who, prompted to all kinds of noisy mirth by the Oxonian and Master Simon, made its old walls ring with their merriment as they played at romping games. I delight in witnessing the gambols of children, and particularly at this happy holiday-season, and could not help stealing out of the drawing room on hearing one of their peals of laughter. . . .

The door suddenly flew open, and a whimsical train came trooping into the room, that might almost have been mistaken for the breaking up of the court of Fairy. That indefatigable spirit, Master Simon, in the faithful discharge of his duties as lord of misrule, had conceived the idea of a Christmas mummery, or masqueing; and having called in to his assistance the Oxonian and the young officer, who were equally ripe for any thing that should occasion romping and merriment, they had carried it into instant effect. The old housekeeper had been consulted; the antique clothes presses and wardrobes rummaged and made to yield up the reliques of finery that had not seen the light for several generations; the younger part of the company had been privately convened from the parlour and hall, and the whole had been bedizzened out, into a burlesque imitation of an antique masque.

Master Simon led the van as "ancient Christmas," quaintly apparel'd in short cloak and ruff, and a hat that might have served for a village steeple, from under which, his nose curved boldly forth, with a frost bitten bloom that seemed the very trophy of a December blast. He was accompanied by the blue-eyed romp, dished up as "Dame mince pie," in the venerable magnificence of faded brocade, long stomacher, peaked hat, and high heeled shoes. The young officer figured in genuine Kendal Green as Robin Hood; the fair Julia in a pretty rustic dress as Maid Marian. The rest of the train had been metamorphosed in various ways; the girls trussed up in the finery of their great grandmothers, and the striplings bewhiskered with burnt cork, and fantastically arrayed to support the characters of Roast Beef,

WILLIAM SIDNEY MOUNT. *Rustic Dance After a Sleigh Ride*. 1830.
Bequest of Martha C. Karolik for the M. and M. Karolik Collection of American Paintings,
1815–1865. Courtesy Museum of Fine Arts, Boston.

JAN STEEN. *The Feast of Saint Nicholas*. Rijksmuseum–Stichting, Amsterdam.

Plum Porridge, and other worthies celebrated in ancient masqueings. The whole was under the control of the Oxonian, in the appropriate characters of Misrule. . . .

It was inspiring to see wild-eyed frolick among the chills and glooms of winter, and old age throwing off its apathy, and catching once more the freshness of youthful enjoyment. I felt an interest in the scene, also, from the consideration that these fleeting customs were posting fast into oblivion; and that this was, perhaps, the only family in England in which the whole of them were still punctiliously observed. There was a quaintness, too, mingled with all this revelry, that gave it a peculiar zest; it was suited to the time and place; and as the old manor house almost reeled with mirth and wassail, it seemed echoing back the joviality of long-departed years.

Holiday Greetings

E. B. WHITE

E. B. White (1899–1985) essayist, poet, humorist, perhaps best known for Charlotte's Web, *or* Stuart Little, *wrote for* The New Yorker *for more than fifty years. This wry, playful Christmas message is from the "Notes and Comment" column.*

December 20, 1952

ROM THIS HIGH midtown hall, undecked with boughs, unfortified with mistletoe, we send forth our tinselled greetings as of old, to friends, to readers, to strangers of many conditions in many places. Merry Christmas to uncertified accountants, to tellers who have made a mistake in addition, to girls who have made a mistake in judgment, to grounded airline passengers, and to all those who can't eat clams! We greet with particular warmth people who wake and smell smoke. To captains of river boats on snowy mornings we send an answering toot at this holiday time. Merry Christmas to intellectuals and other despised minorities! Merry Christmas to the musicians of Muzak and men whose shoes don't fit! Greetings of the season to unemployed actors and the blacklisted everywhere who suffer for sins uncommitted; a holly thorn in the thumb of compilers of lists! Greetings to wives who can't find their glasses and to poets who can't find their rhymes! Merry Christmas to the unloved, the misunderstood, the overweight. Joy to the authors of books whose titles begin with the word "How" (as though they knew)! Greetings to people with a ringing in their

ears; greetings to growers of gourds, to shearers of sheep, and to makers of change in the lonely underground booths! Merry Christmas to old men asleep in libraries! Merry Christmas to people who can't stay in the same room with a cat! We greet, too, the boarders in boarding houses on 25 December, the duennas in Central Park in fair weather and foul, and young lovers who got nothing in the mail. Merry Christmas to people who plant trees in city streets; Merry Christmas to people who save prairie chickens from extinction! Greetings of a purely mechanical sort to machines that think—plus a sprig of artificial holly. Joyous Yule to Cadillac owners whose conduct is unworthy of their car! Merry Christmas to the defeated, the forgotten, the inept; joy to all dandiprats and bunglers! We send, most particularly and most hopefully, our greetings and our prayers to soldiers and guardsmen on land and sea and in the air—the young men doing the hardest things at the hardest time of life. To all such, Merry Christmas, blessings and good luck! We greet the Secretaries-designate, the President-elect; Merry Christmas to our new leaders, peace on earth, goodwill, and good management! Merry Christmas to couples unhappy in doorways! Merry Christmas to all who think they're in love but aren't sure! Greetings to people waiting for trains that will take them in the wrong direction, to people doing up a bundle and the string is too short, to children with sleds and no snow! We greet ministers who can't think of a moral, gagmen who can't think of a joke. Greetings, too, to the inhabitants of other planets; see you soon! And last, we greet all skaters on small natural ponds at the edge of woods toward the end of afternoon. Merry Christmas, skaters! Ring, Steel! Grow red, sky! Die down, wind! Merry Christmas to all and to all a good morrow!

FROM
A Christmas Memory

TRUMAN CAPOTE

*Truman Capote was born in New Orleans and spent most of his childhood
with relatives in Alabama. In this reminiscence we are immersed in the gathering of the
ingredients and the baking of the Christmas fruitcake.*

MAGINE A MORNING in late November. A coming of
winter morning more than twenty years ago. Consider the
kitchen of a spreading old house in a country town. A great
black stove is its main feature; but there is also a big round
table and a fireplace with two rocking chairs placed in front of it. Just today
the fireplace commenced its seasonal roar.

A woman with shorn white hair is standing at the kitchen window. She
is wearing tennis shoes and a shapeless gray sweater over a summery calico
dress. She is small and sprightly, like a bantam hen; but, due to a long youthful illness, her shoulders are pitifully hunched. Her face is remarkable—not
unlike Lincoln's, craggy like that, and tinted by sun and wind; but it is delicate too, finely boned, and her eyes are sherry-colored and timid. "Oh my,"
she exclaims, her breath smoking the windowpane, "it's fruitcake weather!"

The person to whom she is speaking is myself. I am seven; she is sixty-
something. We are cousins, very distant ones, and we have lived together—
well, as long as I can remember. Other people inhabit the house, relatives;
and though they have power over us, and frequently make us cry, we are not,

on the whole, too much aware of them. We are each other's best friend. She calls me Buddy, in memory of a boy who was formerly her best friend. The other Buddy died in the 1880's, when she was still a child. She is still a child.

"I knew it before I got out of bed," she says, turning away from the window with a purposeful excitement in her eyes. "The courthouse bell sounded so cold and clear. And there were no birds singing; they've gone to warmer country, yes indeed. Oh, Buddy, stop stuffing biscuit and fetch our buggy. Help me find my hat. We've thirty cakes to bake."

It's always the same: a morning arrives in November, and my friend, as though officially inaugurating the Christmas time of year that exhilarates her imagination and fuels her heart, announces: "It's fruitcake weather! Fetch our buggy. Help me find my hat."

The hat is found, a straw cartwheel corsaged with velvet roses out-of-doors has faded: it once belonged to a more fashionable relative. Together, we guide our buggy, a dilapidated baby carriage, out to the garden and into a grove of pecan trees. The buggy is mine; that is, it was bought for me when I was born. It is made of wicker, rather unraveled, and the wheels wobble like a drunkard's legs. But it is a faithful object; springtimes, we take it to the woods and fill it with flowers, herbs, wild fern for our porch pots; in the summer, we pile it with picnic paraphernalia and sugar-cane fishing poles and roll it down to the edge of a creek; it has its winter uses, too: as a truck for hauling firewood from the yard to the kitchen, as a warm bed for Queenie, our tough little orange and white rat terrier who has survived distemper and two rattlesnake bites. Queenie is trotting beside it now.

Three hours later we are back in the kitchen hulling a heaping buggy-load of windfall pecans. Our backs hurt from gathering them: how hard they were to find (the main crop having been shaken off the trees and sold by the orchard's owners, who are not us) among the concealing leaves, the frosted, deceiving grass. Caarackle! A cheery crunch, scraps of miniature thunder sound as the shells collapse and the golden mound of sweet oily ivory meat mounts in the milk-glass bowl. Queenie begs to taste, and now and again my friend sneaks her a mite, though insisting we deprive ourselves. "We mustn't, Buddy. If we start, we won't stop. And there's scarcely enough as there is. For thirty cakes." The kitchen is growing dark. Dusk turns the window into a mirror: our reflections mingle with the rising moon as we work by the fireside in the firelight. At last, when the moon is quite high, we toss the final hull into the fire and, with joined sighs, watch it catch flame. The buggy is empty, the bowl is brimful.

We eat our supper (cold biscuits, bacon, blackberry jam) and discuss tomorrow. Tomorrow the kind of work I like best begins: buying. Cherries and citron, ginger and vanilla and canned Hawaiian pineapple, rinds and raisins and walnuts and whiskey and oh, so much flour, butter, so many eggs, spices, flavorings: why, we'll need a pony to pull the buggy home.

But before these purchases can be made, there is the question of money. Neither of us has any. Except for skinflint sums persons in the house occasionally provide (a dime is considered very big money); or what we earn ourselves from various activities: holding rummage sales, selling buckets of hand-picked blackberries, jars of homemade jam and apple jelly and peach preserves, rounding up flowers for funerals and weddings. Once we won seventy-ninth prize, five dollars, in a national football contest. Not that we know a fool thing about football. It's just that we enter any contest we hear about: at the moment our hopes are centered on the fifty-thousand-dollar

Grand Prize being offered to name a new brand of coffee (we suggested "A.M."; and, after some hesitation, for my friend thought it perhaps sacrilegious, the slogan "A.M.! Amen!"). To tell the truth, our only *really* profitable enterprise was the Fun and Freak Museum we conducted in a back-yard woodshed two summers ago. The Fun was a stereopticon with slide views of Washington and New York lent to us by a relative who had been to those places (she was furious when she discovered why we'd borrowed it); the Freak was a three-legged biddy chicken hatched by one of our own hens. Everybody hereabouts wanted to see that biddy: we charged grownups a nickel, kids two cents. And took in a good twenty dollars before the museum shut down due to the decease of the main attraction.

But one way and another we do each year accumulate Christmas savings, a Fruitcake Fund. These moneys we keep hidden in an ancient bead purse under a loose board under the floor under a chamber pot under my friend's bed. The purse is seldom removed from this safe location except to make a deposit, or, as happens every Saturday, a withdrawal; for on Saturdays I am allowed ten cents to go to the picture show. My friend has never been to a picture show, nor does she intend to: "I'd rather hear you tell the story, Buddy. That way I can imagine it more. Besides, a person my age shouldn't squander their eyes. When the Lord comes, let me see Him clear." In addition to never having seen a movie, she has never: eaten in a restaurant, traveled more than five miles from home, received or sent a telegram, read anything except funny papers and the Bible, worn cosmetics, cursed, wished someone harm, told a lie on purpose, let a hungry dog go hungry. Here are a few things she has done, does do: killed with a hoe the biggest rattlesnake ever seen in this county (sixteen rattles), dip snuff (secretly), tame humming-

GRANDMA MOSES. *Christmas at Home.* 1946. © 1996 Grandma Moses Properties Co., N.Y.
*Anna Mary Robertson "Grandma" Moses, the most popular American folk artist of this century, began
painting while in her seventies. Her works celebrate rural traditions and community life.*

birds (just try it) till they balance on her finger, tell ghost stories (we both believe in ghosts) so tingling they chill you in July, talk to herself, take walks in the rain, grow the prettiest japonicas in town, know the recipe for every sort of old-time Indian cure, including a magical wart-remover.

Now, with supper finished, we retire to the room in a faraway part of the house where my friend sleeps in a scrap-quilt-covered iron bed painted rose pink, her favorite color. Silently, wallowing in the pleasures of conspiracy, we take the bead purse from its secret place and spill its contents on the scrap quilt. Dollar bills, tightly rolled and green as May buds. Somber fifty-cent pieces, heavy enough to weight a dead man's eyes. Lovely dimes, the liveliest coin, the one that really jingles. Nickels and quarters, worn smooth as creek pebbles. But mostly a hateful heap of bitter-odored pennies. Last summer others in the house contracted to pay us a penny for every twenty-five flies we killed. Oh, the carnage of August: the flies that flew to heaven! Yet it was not work in which we took pride. And, as we sit counting pennies, it is as though we were back tabulating dead flies. Neither of us has a head for figures; we count slowly, lose track, start again. According to her calculations, we have $12.73. According to mine, exactly $13. "I do hope you're wrong, Buddy. We can't mess around with thirteen. The cakes will fall. Or put somebody in the cemetery. Why, I wouldn't dream of getting out of bed on the thirteenth." This is true: she always spends thirteenths in bed. So, to be on the safe side, we subtract a penny and toss it out the window.

Of the ingredients that go into our fruitcakes, whiskey is the most expensive, as well as the hardest to obtain: State laws forbid its sale. But everybody knows you can buy a bottle from Mr. Haha Jones. And the next day, having completed our more prosaic shopping, we set out for Mr. Haha's

business address, a "sinful" (to quote public opinion) fish-fry and dancing café down by the river. We've been there before, and on the same errand; but in previous years our dealings have been with Haha's wife, an iodine-dark Indian woman with brassy peroxided hair and a dead-tired disposition. Actually, we've never laid eyes on her husband, though we've heard that he's an Indian too. A giant with razor scars across his cheeks. They call him Haha because he's so gloomy, a man who never laughs. As we approach his café (a large log cabin festooned inside and out with chains of garish-gay naked light bulbs and standing by the river's muddy edge under the shade of river trees where moss drifts through the branches like gray mist) our steps slow down. Even Queenie stops prancing and sticks close by. People have been murdered in Haha's café. Cut to pieces. Hit on the head. There's a case coming up in court next month. Naturally these goings-on happen at night when the colored lights cast crazy patterns and the victrola wails. In the daytime Haha's is shabby and deserted. I knock at the door, Queenie barks, my friend calls: "Mrs. Haha, ma'am? Anyone to home?"

Footsteps. The door opens. Our hearts overturn. It's Mr. Haha Jones himself! And he *is* a giant; he *does* have scars; he *doesn't* smile. No, he glowers at us through Satan-tilted eyes and demands to know: "What you want with Haha?"

For a moment we are too paralyzed to tell. Presently my friend half-finds her voice, a whispery voice at best: "If you please, Mr. Haha, we'd like a quart of your finest whiskey."

His eyes tilt more. Would you believe it? Haha is smiling! Laughing, too. "Which one of you is a drinkin' man?"

"It's for making fruitcakes, Mr. Haha. Cooking."

ANDY WARHOL. *Poinsettias*. c. 1982. © The Andy Warhol Foundation for the Visual Arts/ARS, N.Y.
Photograph: The Andy Warhol Foundation, Inc./Art Resource, N.Y.

Henri Matisse. *Nuit de Noel*. Paris, summer–autumn 1952.
Stained-glass window commissioned by LIFE, 1952.
132 3/4 x 54 3/4 x 5/8 in. (332.5 x 139 x 1 cm).
The Museum of Modern Art, New York. Gift of Time, Inc.
Photograph © 1998 The Museum of Modern Art, N.Y.

This sobers him. He frowns. "That's no way to waste good whiskey." Nevertheless, he retreats into the shadowed café and seconds later appears carrying a bottle of daisy-yellow unlabeled liquor. He demonstrates its sparkle in the sunlight and says: "Two dollars."

We pay him with nickels and dimes and pennies. Suddenly, as he jangles the coins in his hand like a fistful of dice, his face softens. "Tell you what," he proposes, pouring the money back into our bead purse, "just send me one of them fruitcakes instead."

"Well," my friend remarks on our way home, "there's a lovely man. We'll put an extra cup of raisins in *his* cake."

The black stove, stoked with coal and firewood, glows like a lighted pumpkin. Eggbeaters whirl, spoons spin round in bowls of butter and sugar, vanilla sweetens the air, ginger spices it; melting, nose-tingling odors saturate the kitchen, suffuse the house, drift out to the world on puffs of chimney smoke. In four days our work is done. Thirty-one cakes, dampened with whiskey, bask on window sills and shelves.

My First Christmas Tree

HAMLIN GARLAND

*Pulitzer prize–winning writer Hamlin Garland, born in 1860, grew up on a
farm in the Midwest before heading east to write for Boston and New York newspapers.
This scene takes place in the 1870s in Wisconsin.*

 WILL BEGIN by saying that we never had a Christmas tree
in our house in the Wisconsin coulee; indeed, my father
never saw one in a family circle till he saw that which I set
up for my own children last year. But we celebrated Christmas in those days, always, and I cannot remember a time when we did not
all hang up our stockings for "Sandy Claws" to fill. As I look back upon those
days it seems as if the snows were always deep, the night skies crystal clear,
and the stars especially lustrous with frosty sparkles of blue and yellow fire—
and probably this was so, for we lived in a Northern land where winter was
usually stern and always long.

I recall one Christmas when "Sandy" brought me a sled, and a horse that
stood on rollers—a wonderful tin horse which I very shortly split in two in
order to see what his insides were. Father traded a cord of wood for the sled,
and the horse cost twenty cents—but they made the day wonderful.

Another notable Christmas Day, as I stood in our front yard, mid-leg deep
in snow, a neighbor drove by closely muffled in furs, while behind his seat his
son, a lad of twelve or fifteen, stood beside a barrel of apples, and as he passed
he hurled a glorious big red one at me. It missed me, but bored a deep, round
hole in the soft snow. I thrill yet with the remembered joy of burrowing for
that delicious bomb. Nothing will ever smell quite as good as that Wine Sap

or Northern Spy or whatever it was. It was a wayward impulse on the part of the boy in the sleigh, but it warms my heart after more than forty years.

We had no chimney in our home, but the stocking-hanging was a ceremony nevertheless. My parents, and especially, my mother, entered into it with the best of humor. They always put up their own stockings or permitted us to do it for them—and they always laughed next morning when they found potatoes or ears of corn in them. I can see now that my mother's laugh had a tear in it, for she loved pretty things and seldom got any during the years that we lived in the coulee.

When I was ten years old we moved to Mitchell County, an Iowa prairie land, and there we prospered in such wise that our stockings always held toys of some sort, and even my mother's stocking occasionally sagged with a simple piece of jewelry or a new comb or brush. But the thought of a family tree remained the luxury of millionaire city dwellers; indeed it was not till my fifteenth or sixteenth year that our Sunday school rose to the extravagance of a tree, and it is of this wondrous festival that I write.

The land about us was only partly cultivated at this time, and our district schoolhouse, a rare little box, was set bleakly on the prairie; but the Burr Oak schoolhouse was not only larger but it stood beneath great oaks as well and possessed the charm of a forest background through which a stream ran silently. It was our chief social center. There of a Sunday a regular preacher held "Divine service" with Sunday school as a sequence. At night—usually on Friday nights—the young people let in "ly-ceums," as we called them, to debate great questions or to "speak pieces" and read essays; and here it was that I saw my first Christmas tree.

I walked to that tree across four miles of moonlit snow. Snow? No, it was a floor of diamonds, a magical world, so beautiful that my heart still aches

with the wonder of it and with the regret that it has all gone—gone with the keen eyes and the bounding pulses of the boy.

Our home at this time was a small frame house on the prairie almost directly west of the Burr Oak grove, and as it was too cold to take the horses out my brother and I, with our tall boots, our visored caps and our long woolen mufflers, started forth afoot defiant of the cold. We left the gate on the trot, bound for a sight of the glittering unknown. The snow was deep and we moved side by side in the grooves made by the hooves of the horses, setting our feet in the shine left by the broad shoes of the wood sleighs whose going had smoothed the way for us.

Our breaths rose like smoke in the still air. It must have been ten below zero, but that did not trouble us in those days, and at last we came in sight of the lights, in sound of the singing, the laughter, the bells of the feast.

It was a poor little building without a tower or bell and its low walls had but three windows on a side, and yet it seemed very imposing to me that night as I crossed the threshold and faced the strange people who packed it to the door. I say "strange people," for though I had seen most of them many times they all seemed somehow alien to me that night. I was an irregular attendant at Sunday school and did not expect a present, therefore I stood against the wall and gazed with open-eyed marveling at the shining pine which stood where the pulpit was wont to be. I was made to feel the more embarrassed by reason of the remark of a boy who accused me of having forgotten to comb my hair.

This was not true, but the cap I wore always matted my hair down over my brow, and then, when I lifted it off invariably disarranged it completely. Nevertheless I felt guilty—and hot. I don't suppose my hair was artistically barbered that night—I rather guess Mother had used the shears—and I can believe that I looked the half-wild colt that I was; but there was

THOMAS BIRCH. *A Winter Sleigh Ride*, c. 1840. Collection of the Brandywine River Museum.
Gift of Hampton C. Randolph, Sr.

MALCAH ZELDIS. *Christmas Street Scene*. Private collection.
Photograph Malcah Zeldis/Art Resource, N.Y.

no call for that youth to direct attention to my unavoidable shagginess.

I don't think the tree had many candles, and I don't remember that it glittered with golden apples. But it was loaded with presents, and the girls coming and going clothed in bright garments made me forget my own looks—I think they made me forget to remove my overcoat, which was a sodden thing of poor cut and worse quality. I think I must have stood agape for nearly two hours listening to the songs, noting every motion of Adoniram Burtch and Asa Walker as they directed the ceremonies and prepared the way for the great event—that is to say, for the coming of Santa Claus himself.

A furious jingle of bells, a loud voice outside, the lifting of a window, the nearer clash of bells, and the dear old Saint appeared (in the person of Stephen Bartle) clothed in a red robe, a belt of sleigh bells, and a long white beard. The children cried out, "Oh!" The girls tittered and shrieked with excitement, and the boys laughed and clapped their hands. Then "Sandy" made a little speech about being glad to see us all, but as he had many other places to visit, and as there were a great many presents to distribute, he guessed he'd have to ask some of the many pretty girls to help him. So he called upon Betty Burtch and Hattie Knapp—and I for one admired his taste, for they were the most popular maids of the school.

They came up blushing and a little bewildered by the blaze of publicity thus blown upon them. But their native dignity asserted itself, and the distribution of the presents began. I have a notion now that the fruit upon the tree was mostly bags of popcorn and "corny copias" of candy, but as my brother and I stood there that night and saw everybody, even the rowdiest boy, getting something we felt aggrieved and rebellious. We forgot that we had come from afar—we only knew we were being left out.

But suddenly, in the midst of our gloom, my brother's name was called,